ABCs to a POSITIVE LIFE

A Simple Guide to a Winning Mindset

Curtis Leong

ABCs to a Positive Life. The Simple Guide to a Winning Mindset
www.ThePositiveLifeBook.com
Copyright © 2020 CURTIS LEONG

ISBN: 978-1-77277-340-8

All rights reserved. No portion of this book may be reproduced mechanically, electronically, or by any other means, including photocopying, without permission of the publisher or author except in the case of brief quotations embodied in critical articles and reviews. It is illegal to copy this book, post it to a website, or distribute it by any other means without permission from the publisher or author.

Limits of Liability and Disclaimer of Warranty
The author and publisher shall not be liable for your misuse of the enclosed material. This book is strictly for informational and educational purposes only.

Warning – Disclaimer
The purpose of this book is to educate and entertain. The author and/or publisher do not guarantee that anyone following these techniques, suggestions, tips, ideas, or strategies will become successful. The author and/or publisher shall have neither liability nor responsibility to anyone with respect to any loss or damage caused, or alleged to be caused, directly or indirectly by the information contained in this book.

Medical Disclaimer
The medical or health information in this book is provided as an information resource only, and is not to be used or relied on for any diagnostic or treatment purposes. This information is not intended to be patient education, does not create any patient-physician relationship, and should not be used as a substitute for professional diagnosis and treatment.

Publisher
10-10-10 Publishing
Markham, ON
Canada

Printed in Canada and the United States of America

Contents

Acknowledgements	ix
Foreword	xiii

Chapter 1: Starting Line — 1
Setting Your Intentions — 1
Your Gear — 3
Looking at Your Past — 5
Getting Clear — 6
Being Bold — 7
Fitting Yourself in Yourself — 8

Chapter 2: 1 2 3 Go — 11
Off to The Race of Your Life — 11
Enjoying the Scenery — 13
Gathering Momentum — 14
Stamina — 15
Keeping Nourished — 18
Staying on the Right Path — 19

Chapter 3: Train Your Brain — 23
Food for Thought — 23
Brain Games — 28
Affirmations — 30
Desserts — 32
Journaling — 33

Chapter 4: An Appropriate Mindset — 39
Setting the Stage — 39
The Right Way to Start the Day — 40
The Right Environment — 42
End of Day Recall — 44
Recalling Your Best Moments of the Day, Week, and Month — 47

Chapter 5: Being Positive with Others — 49
Using Clearing Techniques — 49
Replace Your Thoughts with Positive Ones — 51
Using Positive Words — 53
Dealing with Negative People — 54
How to Be the New You — 57

Chapter 6: Your Why to A Positive Life — 59
Discovering Your Positive Lifestyle — 59
Whom to Look Up To — 61
Using Self-Hypnosis to Increase Your Mindset — 62
Writing Your Own Affirmations — 67
The One Thing That Has Made You Change — 69

Chapter 7: The Right Way To Self-Talk — 71
Keeping the Self-Talk Positive — 71
Affirmations — 72
Ho Oponopono — 74
Being Optimistic — 77
Self-Confidence — 79

Chapter 8: Leading The Way — 81
Believe in Yourself — 81
Getting Out of Your Way — 83
Inspiring Others to Be Positive — 84
Knowing Your Best Points/Self-Assessment — 86

Chapter 9: Knowing Your Finish Line	**89**
Finding Your Goals	89
Knowing Your Route	92
Drawing Your Map	93
Chapter 10: You Are A Winner	**97**
Maintain Your Beliefs	100
Making Your Morning Routine	101
End of Day Winner Circle of Greatness	103
Congratulations	107
About the Author	109

I dedicate this book to Reta Leong and London Leong who have encouraged me to keep a positive attitude through difficult times. Love you to infinity XO.

Acknowledgements

I would like to thank my mom, Marion Gillingham, for encouraging me to be my personal best. It was her great examples that have made me the positive man I am today. Mom, it is because of your wisdom and dedication to your children that I have the confidence and great work ethic I have today, which is why I was able to finish this book. Thanks Mom! Thank you Carl Gillingham for your great attitude and your dedication to keeping Marion happy. You are a good role model and have encouraged me to be a better man.

I would like to thank my wife, Reta Leong, for all her admiration and her support in helping me achieve my goals. Thank you Reta for keeping the house in fine order and for being the best wife I could have ever have. I love you! XO. I knew that you were awesome from the first day we met.

I give a big hug and kiss to London Leong. She is the greatest daughter a dad could have. London, you are an amazing girl who always brings joy and happiness to me and your mom. You have inspired me to have a better life, from the day I saw you born. Thank you! Keep being your best!

I give big thanks to Roxane, Stuart, Emily, and Ethan Hendrie, for their amazing help with this book and for being a great source of inspiration and guidance. Their continued support of my family and me is appreciated.

I am grateful to Harry Leong for being the best dad he could be. Harry, I appreciate what you did when Reta and I first moved to Ontario. Thanks to Andy, Chris, Jeff and Phil, for being great brothers.

I am grateful for Joy Scott, Shelby Scott, and Breanna Tokarz for their enthusiasm and excitement for me when I decided to write my book. Their continued support is most welcome and keeps the positive vibe going.

I would like to thank the people I work with at Aerloc. Dave Dendecker, my boss. Chris Combs for his encouraging words, "When is the book done." Luke Vanlunana for his enthusiastic personality and great support that inspired me to keep up my positive attitude; Cam Hollings for his great stories of fish, hunting and life; Scott Dewerd for his continuing jokes and buggery that make me laugh. Peter Koopman, Matt Baily, Matt Hurst, Kalvin Latto, Craig Cowell, Blair Tuffs, Clayton Hudder, Dave Cole, Steve Sims, Cam Dalio, and all the other employees that I have had the pleasure to work with over the years; the friendly drivers, Richard, John, Julio and the many people that work tirelessly in the shop to keep the installers busy; Tracy, who tirelessly keeps a great attitude whenever I call or need something done. Thank you. I appreciate all of the people in the office that do the measuring, the paperwork, the drawings, and the many other activities that make the work we do come together.

I am happy to have great in-laws, Mike and Ruth Kearns. Their amazing attitudes to live a happy and joyful life have made me feel great. Their support and dedication is amazing. Thank you, David Kearns, for being a great brother in-law. Your cooking skills are amazing. Thank you Lauren Coughlin and Peggy Noble for being supportive and helpful. I would like to thank the rest of my wife's family who are not listed as there are too many to write down.

I appreciated Patty for her great meditation and spiritual inspirations that have come through when I have attended meditation nights. I am glad to have met great people that came out each week; you are all great. I have continued with the meditations that I have learned from Patty over the years and they have always been very helpful with my self-development.

Foreword

Would you like to have more success and happiness in your life? In *ABCs to a Positive Life,* author Curtis Leong shows you how to achieve this, simply by exploring your values. The values of relationship, caring and doing the right thing are needed in both family and business today, and Curtis argues that, without them, your personal positive life is looking at an inescapable downfall. This book will encourage you to challenge your beliefs, find your values, learn to be yourself, and guide your positive life accordingly. By being truthful to yourself and others, you will find *huge* power and success.

ABCs to a Positive Life is filled with techniques and ideas that will help you achieve new levels of inspiration and clarity in your life.

I have had the pleasure of meeting Curtis at several events and seminars over the years, and have always been impressed by his positive attitude. If you want to be better, feel better! *ABCs to a Positive Life* will guide you to believe in yourself, live a positive lifestyle, and encourage others to do the same.

Raymond Aaron
New York Times Bestselling Author

Chapter 1

Starting Line

"The secret of getting ahead is getting started."
Mark Twain

"There's no way to become great overnight, but in the marathon of success, it takes a lot of intention to see you through each day of the journey."
Lewis Howes

Setting Your Intentions

When you've set meaningful intentions you know where you're coming from. In setting intentions based on your highest values, your life becomes full of purpose, because you understand what's important to you. Powerful intention statements are shaped from knowing what's important to you.

To get your intention let's first look at the meaning.

Intention (noun) an act or instance of determining mentally upon some action or result.

So let's think about what our intention is. What do you want to achieve, or what do you need to do to change your personal direction. Conscious mind and subconscious mind what are they. By definition....

Conscious (adjective)
1. Aware of one's own existence, sensations, thoughts, surroundings, etc.
2. Fully aware of or sensitive to something (often followed by of).

Subconscious. (adjective)
1. Existing or operating in the mind beneath or beyond consciousness

A story of mine would be when my wife and I decided to start saving for our first house. First, we looked at where we were financially, what we needed to do for savings, and how much. During this time we were in debt and had no real idea of how to get started with the saving part. I was working at a restaurant, and I meet one of the other employees that happened to be starting in life insurance and an investing venture. I got lots of info from her. My wife and I decided to meet up and get the full run-down on her business. Initially I was not going to do it, but by compiling information and easy number crunching we did it. So, for the next 3 years, we saved and budgeted to get to our goal. Did we get there? Close enough to get the down payment for our house. The next thing is to write your intentions down on paper. I found this to be like a letter, requesting to get what you want. When we did our writing, it was a budget plan and the amount we needed to save.

Next is to keep what you have written down in a spot or spots where you can see it every day. This will help ingrain that intention into your subconscious mind.

We had ours on the fridge and at our bedsides.

Your intentions should be done daily. You should act on them to demonstrate commitment, and amazing things will then begin to happen. Our intentions can give us the fortitude for dealing with tough times.

Here are some other examples of how you can use intentions. Before you get out of bed in the morning you can intend to have a fun or productive day. Before you leave the house, you can intend to have quality time with your family. Before you start your car, you can intend to have a safe ride to work. Before you enter your workplace, you can intend to learn something new or be helpful. Before the meeting begins, you can intend to be brilliant and calm.

Here are four steps that will help you set up your intentions.

1. Make a plan – Get clear about something you want, and write it down. You can set up for daily, weekly, monthly and yearly plans.
2. Be accountable – Share your intention with someone, in a way that will sportively hold you accountable to taking action (a coach/mentor would be best).
3. Show commitment – Do something today to demonstrate your commitment to your intention.
4. Take action – Acknowledge that you did what you said you would, and then take the next step. Be sure to have small rewards to keep you in action, to keep you moving forward.

Setting intentions is a great way to work on centering yourself and focusing on things you'd like to achieve. The purpose of intentions is to help focus your behaviour on making you a better person and working toward the things that bring you joy and fulfillment. Start by working on your focus, and then turn that focus into specific intentions. Follow through with your intentions by referring back to them and using them to guide your thoughts and plans.

Your Gear

So, what is the gear you need? First, ask yourself " Self, what do I want to believe in? What do I want? What can I have?" You need to write these points down, so please grab a pen and paper. Journaling will help you to keep your intentions and daily thoughts in focus.

When you do this exercise for the first time, it will be challenging. You can think about your personal beliefs and, what you stand for, and ask friends and family what they see in you. Their view of you can help guide you with this exercise.

Next, what do you want in your personal life, business life, relationship, spiritual life?

What can you have in your life? This is where you can bring it all together to make it work for you. This is the point where it becomes powerful. How you are thinking is simply where your intentions make the difference.

This is part of your gear. You can use a note book or a nice journal. You can use a pen or pencil that you like or a fancy one. I use a note book and a nice pen. I write in my journal daily, usually in the morning. You can do it at night to reflect on your day and create your intentions for the next day. It can be a simple intention to have a great day, or it can be more complicated, about what you want to accomplish for the month. Just let your mind and pen flow with it. Here are some tips to help you:

- Time yourself. Give yourself a time limit of 5 – 10 minutes to get your thoughts down on paper. This will make it easier to start each day.

- Use paper only. This will allow you to slow down and really immerse yourself in the creative process of journaling. It's a nice break from our screen-driven world.

- Date your entries. This allows you to look back and reflect on what's been happening in your life, and how you have felt at different times in your life. This can be incredibly insightful. It also shows you gaps between entries, which is helpful to reflect on and keep track of.

- Be truthful. Your journal is yours and yours alone. Allow yourself to write down the truth about what's going on in your life, and how you are feeling about it. Don't talk yourself out of accepting what you are feeling. Take your time, go slow and let the truth flow out.

- Re-read your entries. There is something important in every journal entry you write, even if you don't see/know it when you are writing it. Always keep your journal entries and re-read them. They will offer lots of insight at a time you need it most.

Looking at Your Past

To get to know how to move forward, reflect on your past thinking and habits. How did you used to think? What were some of the difficulties you faced? How did they make you feel at the time, and how does it make you feel today? What habits did you have? For example when someone said something negative, did you get mad? Or did you let it go?

There were times in your past that were bad. You can turn the negative moments around by being brave and learning from them. You can remember the bad times, but learn to make better moments in the future. The best way to make sure your history doesn't repeat itself is by making better choices now.

Looking at your past will help you to never forget where you came from. It will give you great stories to share with others. If you a have problem remembering some of the details, ask trusted family and friends to jog your memory. I am sure they will give you some great details. Also, you could keep a journal to help you to remember today, for your future self. Your past experiences also make you who you are today, which is great.

Your past can be used in some way. You can help others with your experiences, and have valuable insight on situations that you have encountered, to give someone else a better future, including yourself. Looking at your past tells you how well you have been working on your strengths and weaknesses. Have you heard of the definition of insanity? It's doing the same thing over and over again, expecting different results. This can lead to a monotonous cycle that gets you into a rut. Thankfully this is not you, and it is great that you are improving yourself. Looking at the past in this way will tell you if you have been working toward your goals or not. Based on this analyzation, you now have a good idea of what kind of improvements need to be made. Keep working towards your goals; you are amazing! Keep it up. If you find yourself in the opposite direction, make the improvements now. instead of "someday!!"

Getting Clear

Getting clear with yourself, means to get rid of your limiting beliefs or other personal obstacles. What are limiting beliefs? How do they affect your life?

A limiting belief is a false belief that a person could acquire as a result of making an incorrect conclusion about something in their life. For example, telling yourself : " I want to ask for a raise but I don't think now is the right time." Are you being practical and pragmatic, or are you fearful that the boss might say no? Do you think that they will see you as being greed or if they felt you were worth more, they'd have already offered it to you? There are a lot more of these types of thoughts that you could have.

The problem with limiting beliefs is that they force you to live below your potential. Here is a another example to help you understand limiting beliefs: If there is a box that weights 10 Kg, but you believe that it weighs 100 Kg you might not even try to move it, because you think that you can't. So, this example shows how limiting beliefs can prevent you from lifting the box, even though you have the ability to lift it.

So, how do you get rid of limiting beliefs? First, question the limiting beliefs. If a friend told you that the box weighted 100 Kg, ask him some questions. Did you try to lift it yourself? Who told you that it weighs 100 Kg? What is the proof? The limiting belief might be just a point of view. If your friend is physically weak, then he might be saying that the box is heavy because it is heavy for him, but it may not necessarily be heavy for you. This proves that limiting beliefs might be the point of view of another person, and not necessarily the facts. To overcome a limiting belief, try it yourself. As in the example, try to lift the box yourself. Did you manage to lift it? You can ask others if they have lifted it, and how they did it. You need to prove to yourself that you can do, it and be persistent to get to the truth until you personally prove it false.

So limiting beliefs can prevent you from reaching your potential. Winning in life means having an ability to locate and eliminate your limiting beliefs, to become your own success.

Being Bold

Being bold is to have self-confidence. What is self-confidence, and where does it come from? These are two great questions to help you become more self-confident. Self-confidence means to feel good about yourself and your capabilities. Self-confidence benefits you in a powerful way; it is a good feeling that makes you happier and more successful. You can develop and maintain it in any situation or circumstance. You can do this because it comes from within you, and not from other people around you.

Where does self-confidence come from? Self-confidence comes from your abilities. For this reason, you can think of self-confidence as confidence because it comes from *things you* CAN do in any situations or circumstance, regardless of what others want you to do.

More specifically, self-confidence comes from powerful abilities that you possess: For one, your ability to think positively about yourself and your capabilities, secondly, your ability to be certain that you are someone of positive value, who has powerful capabilities (whether others doubt or disagree with you); thirdly, your ability to continue to thinks positively about yourself and your capabilities, in any situation or circumstance. To maintain your self-confidence, recognize that you already have all the abilities that make you more self-confident, and that you can keep developing and using those abilities to get greater confidence in yourself.

Here is an example of self-confidence: It is common and normal for people to be nervous about public speaking, especially the first time, but a self-confident person will not feel as nervous or anxious. This is because the individual knows, without a doubt, that they CAN deliver the speech that they wrote, and know without a doubt, that they can accept, handle, learn, gain, and benefit from any outcome. Your confidence is tested when you deliver a speech, the crowd could boo you or tell you to get off the stage. Because of your self-confidence, you continue with your speech, with your head held up high. Also this experience is of great positive value, because it will help you to become better at giving speeches in the future, and continue to build your self-confidence.

Fitting Yourself into Yourself

To be authentic is to be comfortable with who you are, to stand up for your values, and to know what and how you can contribute to life.

We are born authentic, but the hard knocks of life can mess us up. It is a long journey, but you can get back to your innocent self-acceptance, by using tools and having more understanding . You can secure a hard-won self-acceptance in your adult life.

ABCs to a Positive Life

There are three beliefs that have kept me going, and which help me to fit myself in to myself. First, I honour my body. I appreciate it for what it is. I know it's not perfect, but I have done some amazing things with it, and it has done amazing things for me. Some of the things I do to honour my body are that I stay fit. I do a morning stretching routine and some push ups, sit-ups, and chin ups. I eat as healthy as I can with lots of fruit, vegetables, water, and white meats and fish. What ways can you find to honour your body? Brainstorm some ideas ,and find out what motivates you. Write them down, and do some of the ideas. Find the ones that work for you, and that you find easy.

Second, keep the candles burning. Keep hope alive. Seek out stories of people and there kindness, and examples of humanity helping each other. Cheer for the underdogs, and help those you can. I have found that this makes me feel that there is still good in the world, and that not everyone is out to get each other or to ruin things. What stories have inspired you? What acts of kindness have you done? What act of kindness has someone done for you?

Thirdly, nurture your own spirit; do things that strengthen your inner peace. Have time alone to reflect, pray, meditate, do yoga, or tai chi, walk, etc. It is necessary to take care of your inner-self. The more authentic, peaceful, and self-accepting you are, the more compassion you can offer to others. I have started to meditate using muse. This is a device that monitors your brain activity. With the app and the device you can get into a deeper meditation. I am really enjoying using it. What I like is that you can pick out different meditation themes, such as heart-centred mindfulness. It has 5 exercises that guide you through heart felt qualities of mindfulness, gratitude, curiosity, wonder and compassion. The other one is with Deepak Chopra as your guide. There are 3 exercises on how to observe the breath, essential nature, and inner quiet. Another one is on having a mindful life, which helps you strengthen your focused attention. This one has 4 exercises that guide you, using simple skills to strengthen your focused attention. Muse Essential has 10 lessons to introduce you to meditation. You can pick out different soundscapes.

From this. do you think you can fit yourself into yourself? Will you start to do some of the above suggestions?

Now onward with your positive life.

Chapter 2

1, 2, 3 Go

"The key to change... is to let go of fear."
Rosanne Cash

Off to the Race of Your Life

The stadium is buzzing with eager anticipation. Cheers echo through the crowd as we watch the runners gather at the starting line. The starter calls, "On your marks," and each runner lines up in their lane. At the sound of the gun, the runners are off like rockets, pacing themselves for the long race ahead.

Here you are in the race of your life. How do you see it? Who are you racing against? How long will it take? There are so many questions we ask ourselves every day. It's time to live your life differently.

Let's start our day by doing daily journaling, having your morning routine written down: stretching, getting your body moving first thing in the morning, reading inspirational or self-improvement books/materials, using meditation and intention to keep believing in what you're doing.

Some of the things I do for my morning routine are to, wake up early, write my book or read, stretch, do some push-ups and sit ups, eat breakfast and drink a green smoothly, do meditation with my muse headset, and journaling. I find that this makes the day better, because I am starting off on the right foot. So if you start in the right frame of mind, your daily race will be more enjoyable.

If this is too much to start with, you can start off with small steps. You could start with affirmations in the morning, and again before you go to bed. You can build up your routine over time; just keep your goal in mind. There is more on how to set and achieve your goals, later in the book.

Just by thinking about how to change your life, your subconscious mind will start to search for ways to improve and change your life for the better.

Here are some points to help you:

- Stop complaining, complaining is a waste of time. It allows undesirable thoughts to take over, and makes the complainer look negative. Not only does the complainer waste energy, so do the people that are listening to the complainer. Limit negativity to increase positivity. You need to re-frame the negativity if it is affecting you.

- Be grateful; Gratitude is a virtue that brings great enjoyment to life. Take time each day to be grateful for life experiences. For example, the comfortable bed you sleep in, the smell of coffee brewing in the morning, the warm house you are in, and other regular blessings of life. Remember that not everyone has access to these small pleasures. Even more so, people don't take the time to fully experience the small pleasures that fill their lives. Don't be one of them. Stop and take time to be grateful. Begin by writing a gratitude list at the end of each day. Soon, it will become second nature to be grateful for the people and experiences in your life.

- Smile often. Smiling has a positive effect on mood and perceived energy levels. The act of smiling can improve your attitude in a matter of seconds. Try it the next time a bad mood comes along, to immediately reverse it. Smiles project happiness and confidence by softening other facial gestures. Not only can smiling improve the mood of surrounding people, but it can also be heard. For example, most people can determine whether the person they are speaking to over the phone is smiling by the tone and rhythm of their voice. Keep on smiling.

Enjoying the Scenery

If you want to enjoy the scenery, remember to keep your eyes and your heart open. The opportunities are there. With your new sense of awareness, you will see the right opportunities magically show up. Keep your goals in mind, and you will see and find them. So, as the saying goes stop, and smell the roses. As on a long drive to a nice place, you need to stop and see the different scenery of each city or town along your route. This will bring happy and positive memories. Enjoy the great things that you see, and let the not-so-important things be forgotten.

Have you ever driven fast? Were you able to remember what you saw? Life can be like that too. We have a tenancy to be in a rush or hurried by work or friends. The everyday hustle can keep you distracted enough to forget to think about yourself. This is can be unhealthy for you. This part of the book I hope can help you find the time to take a break for you. Enjoy the scenery!

This is also a way to take some me time. Most people feel the need to be going all the time. If we are not working and putting our energy into something, we believe we are wasting time. You may feel taking time for yourself is a waste. However, going long periods without time for yourself may cost you in the end. Stress and the inability to just enjoy a little time out has very real health and psychological effects.

Some of them can include: heart attacks, strokes, asthma, obesity, diabetes, headaches, gastrointestinal problems, lessened immune function. Mentally, people may experience mental fatigue, insomnia, confusion, poor concentration, depression, anxiety, and increased irritability. Just like we need sleep, we need our personal time out. The biggest reason to have time to yourself is to avoid the negative consequences of not doing so. But more then that, "me" time can make you a better person both inside and out.

When you spend your time filling other people's cups, it's likely yours will run empty. Sometimes, especially when we are tired, we may become angry about giving so much. Sometimes we minimize our need for "me" time by thinking about how we are denying attention to other things that are important to us, such as, our family, out friends, our gym time, the lawn or whatever else. We feel selfish taking the needed time out when there's so much left to do. However, if you run yourself to the ground you are not going to much help to anyone, and you won't be able to fully engage in your activities anyway. Your health is vital, and if you think these obligations can't succeed without you, thing of what might happen if you became sick and have to set them aside for a longer amount of time. You need a little time to recharge your batteries.

Gathering Momentum

Now that you are moving in the right direction with your positive life, let's keep it going throughout the day by remembering your intention of the day, keeping it at the top of your mind. Let's keep building on that momentum so that, like a rock rolling down a hill it gathers more momentum. Some of the ways to do that is by speaking positive to others and to yourself. Keep affirmations on your phone, setting the alarm to remind yourself to read them and reflect. It's up to you to stay on the river of relativity. Maintaining momentum can be a challenge, especially when you are in a procrastinating mood. A good way to keep your momentum up is by having a schedule and a productive environment as well as minimizing distractions.

Breathe deeply; stretch out the diaphragm with deep breathing. Muscular stress, heart rate, and blood pressure can all be reduced in a few deep breaths. Breathing can help centre attention, and focus the mind. You can do this when starting to meditate. It is also a practice that pregnant women use with Lamaze. This aids with pain management during the birthing process. Shallow breathing is a response to stress and fear. A method to use is the 6-2-6 method: Breathe in for a count of 6; hold for 2; then exhale for 6. Reduce stress, enjoy your positive life, and take time to breathe deeply.

Take a walk; take a walk every day. Enjoy the time alone, the environment, and the ability to move your body. Daily walks help clear the mind, and connect you with nature. Walking provides an opportunity for connecting with friends or family members. Get out of your house or office, and get some fresh air. Walking is the most basic of physical activities, and contributes to physical and mental health. This exercise can help build cardio endurance, and is great for lower body joint health. With little risk of injury, walking provides a great opportunity to enjoy life.

For some other you might enjoy running, swimming or bike riding. These activities will give you the same effects as walking would. It depends on your fitness level. Just enjoy the time alone be positive to yourself.

Stamina

Stamina is the strength and energy needed to exert oneself for an extended period of time. The word most commonly refers to the exertion needed for physical activities like exercise and sports. However, stamina can also refer to the mental exertion needed to perform a task or get through a difficult situation. Improving either type of stamina is a great choice.

To keep going when life gets tough is hard. I have worked in very negative environments in my life. I never knew it at that time. Once you realize how to start to improve yourself, you begin to see things in a different light. This is where stamina will be used to keep you on the path to self-improvement. What I have found that has worked is to keep the positive events in my life at the front of my mind. Also, keep reading your affirmations and your goals on your phone, or have them written down on pieces of paper close to your work space, in your car, and in various locations around your home, and this will keep you going. I have found affirmations in books and, of course, on the internet which I like and have inspired me. You can add new ones and replace some as you see fit for your situation. Also it would help to change locations every once in a while. Keeps you from turning a blind eye to them. Much like when you are driving and you all of a sudden you realize you are in a different spot on the road. When you set goals and achieve them, it helps you to keep going. We will go through goal setting, in another chapter. Also going to seminars, workshops and boot camps will help. By being around great people and learning new things will give you the boost you need.

Here are some factors that will help build your mental stamina:

- Eat right: Proper nutrition is key to increasing mental stamina. The brain has a judge demand for energy and nutrients to function well. Some foods that will benefit you are almonds, blueberries and walnuts. According to brain experts these work. They are rich in omega-3 fatty acids, and good amounts of antioxidants in the blue berries.

- Adequate sleep. Of course. Your brain needs rest. During sleep, the brain gets some me time that it utilizes to rebuild its neural networks and do some mental spring cleaning. Missing out on sleep takes away this healing time. This affects your mental stamina as well as keenness.

ABCs to a Positive Life

- Exercise. Rest and exercise, both are very important for the brain. By doing both you improve your mental stamina. By exercising for at least 30 minutes every day. It keeps our brain working at its optimum capacity.

- Manage your stress. We have all heard about the debilating effects of stress on our minds and bodies. Stress is a major mental depressor. A great suggestion is to use visualization exercises to keep this monster tame. All you have to do is to imagine that you are in a soothing place whenever you are overwhelmed. Also meditation and relax consciously each muscle group from your toes to your head while meditating.

- Practice deep breathing. Deep abdominal breathing fills up your longs with oxygen that improves brain function. A regular deep breathing practice is excellent for upping mental stamina and acuity. It also relaxes your mind, which will improve your mental stamina.

- Do one thing at a time. If you really want to improve your focus and mental stamina, it is important to narrow in on one thing at a time, see it through to completion, and then take on something else.

- Drink lots of water. 70% of your body is water and your body requires lots of it to function. Try to drink as much as two liters of water a day, to make sure that your body and its organs are being replenished and rejuvenated. I like to drink filtered water that takes out most of the toxins out of the tap water.

- Limit your internet usage. A study recently linked the increased availability of high-speed internet services has a diminished attention capacity. Some solutions that could help are having a timer on your phone or home computer to limit your time on the internet. So you can take a break from it. You could delete the apps that are causing you the most temptation. You can also add notification blockers on your computer so you don't get distracted. You could even have a better idea.

Keeping Nourished

Keeping nourished which is to eat healthy and have a balanced diet, food is the fuel your body gets its energy from. A well-balanced diet keeps your body healthy and energized, raising your stamina.

A suggestion for a well-balanced diet would be:

- A low fat diet that includes plenty of fruits, vegetables, and lean meats. There are many types of diets you can follow ask your doctor for the best one for you.

- To keep your body steadily supplied with energy throughout the day, eat several small meals rather than one or two large meals. Snack on fruits, raw vegetables, nuts, and other lean proteins between meals. Carry high energy fruit and nut mixtures with you during times of extended performance, such as hiking, and cycling, or at seminars, workshop and boot camps.

- Stay hydrated. The health benefits of drinking lots of water are numerous. For example, it can help you lose weight, prevent kidney stones and much more. Water can also increase stamina by fighting muscle fatigue. Muscle tissue that is under-hydrated can under-perform. So, keep your stamina up by drinking water a few hours before strenuous exercise and during your work out as well. If you happen to be starting on a long distance run or an extended exercise, have plenty of fluids with you so, that they will be available to you later.

Drinking your 8 cups of water daily, is just the beginning, your body, mind, and spirit also needs food. (yes you will pee more). For the body and mind, you need a healthy diet.

I do a stretching sequence and push ups, and sit ups, and I make green smoothies every morning. I have reduced my sugar and salt intake. I follow the caveman diet plan. You can choose the one you like, it is about being disciplined. Pick a healthy diet that you like and can follow. For my mind, I take supplements like fish oil, ginkgo biloba, and regular multi vitamins. I read inspirational books every night. In the morning, I like to play brain games and do a five minute meditation, it gets me ready for the day. The two brain games, I like are Luminosity and Elevate. It's a great way to activate the brain to start thinking. If you like crosswords or Sudoku these are great choices to activating your mind.

For my spirit, I like to do meditation every night. The first step is to get in to a relaxed state. How I do this is by taking a breath in for 6 - 8 seconds, holding it for 2 seconds, and then slowly breathing out for 6 - 8 seconds. I repeat this three times. Then I follow up with a guided meditation during which time I will fall asleep. You tube has lots of meditations you can use. Also I have used binaural beat meditation, which I found accelerates the meditation process. In the morning I use my muse headset to meditate. It has an app that helps me to focus deeper on my meditation state. I enjoy this time because it helps me to focus on the tasks of the day, and to remain in a calm state throughout the day. I also attend church regularly, and read the bible for inspiration.

Staying on the Right Path

To keep, your journey of a positive life going in a good direction, it's up to you. I have had great days, good days, and some bad days during my journey. I have made the decision to keep on this path, no matter what happens in my life. I need to be my most happy, outgoing, and best self I can be. This decision has helped me even in the worst of times. It continues to keep me going every day. At first, it was hard; but, by keeping at it I have built my stamina, and kept my momentum, which help me enjoy the scenery and stay on the right path.

Each day is different. You need to have goals to help you stay on the path that you have chosen. I like to write mine down and put reminders around my house to keep me going. I have a tendency to forget 'where I am in my journey. With the goals being present and readily available, it is easier to stay on the path that you are on. Ask yourself some questions: What do I want? Where do I want to be finically, spiritually, and in my relationships, in the next year, 5 years, or 10 years?

Here is a story of a shark. During a research experiment a marine biologist placed a shark into a large holding tank and then released several small bait fish in to the tank. As expected, the shark quickly attacked and ate the smaller fish. The marine biologist then inserted a strong piece of clear fiberglass into the tank, creating two separate partitions. He then put the shark on one side of the fiberglass and a new set of bait fish on the other.

Again, the shark quickly attacked. This time however, the shark slammed into the fiberglass divider and bounced off. Undeterred, the shark kept repeating this behavior every few minutes to no avail. Meanwhile, the bait fish swam around unharmed in the second portion. Eventually, about an hour into the experiment, the shark gave up.

This experiment was repeated several dozen times over the next few weeks. Each time, the shark got less aggressive and made fewer attempts to attack the bait fish, until eventually the shark got tired of hitting the fiberglass divider and simply stopped attacking altogether. The marine biologist then removed the fiberglass divider, but the shark didn't attack. The shark was trained to believe a barrier existed between it and the bait fish, so the bait fish swam wherever they wished, free from harm.

The moral: Many of us, after experiencing setbacks and failures, emotionally give up and stop trying. Like the shark in the story, we believe that because we were unsuccessful in the past, we will always be unsuccessful. In other works, we continue to see a barrier in our heads, even when no 'real' barrier exists between where we are and where we want to go.

This is why this book will help you get through your barriers.

In the space below write some ideas down. Do it now!!!!

Awesome! You are doing great!

Chapter 3

Train Your Brain

"You have to train your brain to be positive just like you work out your body."
Shawn Anchor

Food for Thought

What *does food for thought mean?* It means learning new information that you never thought was important to think about. It enables you to have greater intelligence in every aspect of life while feeding your mind.

What foods can you use to think? Here are some ideas that can help you: First, you should keep your thoughts positive, secondly you can do daily affirmations; and third, try to hang out with as many positive people as you can.

Meditation and self-hypnosis techniques, used in combination with positive thoughts, can really help integrate the ideas into your psyche. There are hundreds of books on the power of positivity. It includes physical and spiritual wellness, as well as health in our relationships, finances, and many other areas of our lives. Here is a list of ten books that you should read or own, which can help you with your positive life journey.

The Alchemist by Paulo Coelhos: The wisdom that The Alchemist shares is simple yet profound. Santiago, a shepherd boy, goes on a quest from his home in Spain, in search of treasure hidden inside an ancient Egyptian pyramid. Meeting an alchemist, a Gypsy woman, and a man who calls himself king, Santiago is guided on his journey to uncover the treasures found within. This book brings a realization of the value contained in our hearts, minds, and dreams.

The Power of Positive Thinking, by Norman Vincent Peale: Is one of the most recognized positive thinking books in the world. Norman has inspired and helped millions of people realize that their dreams lie within the ability to practice full faith in everyday actions. Through his positive, practical techniques, Norman describes how to have a new level of, *oomph in life* to manifest your hopes and ambitions.

Think and grow rich, by Napoleon Hill: Think and Grow Rich has sold over 20million copies. In the story, Napoleon dedicated 20 years of his life studying and interviewing 500 of the most successful people at the time. Thomas Edison, Henry Ford, and Andrew Carnegie were all subjects of Napoleon's diligent research. This book has had a tremendous influence on us. It did so much for the whole field of personal development and positive thinking.

As A Man Thinketh, by James Allen. In this book, James follows the simple yet profound premise that your thoughts create your life. If you have a practice of positive thinking, all the world softens toward you and is ready to help you. This bolsters the belief that you attract whether it is that you are thinking, whether it be love or fear-based thoughts, your subconscious delivery system serves as a catalyst of physical manifestation.

Psycho- Cybernetics, by Maxwell Malts: Combines cognitive behavioral techniques with cybernetics, to define the intricate workings of our mind-body connection and how it serves as the core in attaining our goals in life. Maltz worked with many of his clients to make their goals of a positive outcome occur through the visualization of that outcome. The world's leading experts in self-help and personal development, like Tony Robbins, Zig Ziglar, and Brian Tracy, have used the work of Maxwell Maltz as a foundation for their own teachings.

The Magic, By Rhonda Byrne: Rohonda Byne's, books *The Secret*, *The Power*, and *The Magic* have garnered world attention and sparked a global awakening. *The Magic* takes us one step further through, and shows us that gratitude is the key to changing your life.

The Magic takes you on a life changing, 28-day journey, with a follow-up in each chapter that contains special exercises to help you practice gratitude. We have found that this book and the positive thinking practices contained within will not only assist in changing the way you think, but will also set your dreams and desires into motion.

The Charge-Activating the 10 Human Drives That Make You Feel Alive, by Brendon Burchard: This book will take you on a personal journey to live a more impassioned life. It will teach you how to embrace change and challenges, how to discover your outlets for creative expression, and the value of contributing and aligning ourselves to personal goals or aspirations.

The Charge challenges each of us to become more passionate in life, through discovering your creativity and expressing it in your own unique way. We love this book, and you surely will too!

The Power of Now, by Eckhart Tolle: Brings understandable spirituality to every person, especially those with a Western world-view. The simple language Eckhart Tolle uses in this book simply cuts through falsehood, bringing a deep meaning to the everyday experiences in life, along with a self-realization of the true importance that the NOW contains. We highly recommend this book and would love to hear what you think.

The Four Agreements, by Don Miguel Ruiz: Is a life-changing book, whose ideas come from the ancient Toltec wisdom of the native people of Southern Mexico. The Toltec were known "people of knowledge", and Ruiz's family was firmly emboldened with this knowledge.

The simple ideas of *The Four Agreements* provide a guide-map for living a positive life. Here are *The Four Agreements*, and what they mean according to Ruiz

- **Be impeccable with your word**
  Speak with integrity. Say only what you mean. Avoid using the word to speak against yourself or to gossip about others. Use the power of your word in the direction of truth and love.

- **Don't take anything personally**
  Nothing others do is because of you. What others say and do is a projection of their own reality, their own dream. When you are immune to the opinions and actions of others, you won't be the victim of needless suffering.

- **Don't make assumptions**
  Find the courage to ask questions and to express what you really want. Communicate with others as clearly as you can to avoid misunderstandings, sadness, and drama. With just this one agreement, you can completely transform your life.

- **Always do your best**
  Your best is going to change from moment to moment; it will be different when you are healthy as opposed to sick. Under any circumstance, simply do your best and you will avoid self-judgment, self-abuse, and regret.

As you make these four agreements, your life will dramatically change. Integrating them into your being and every area of your life will soon become a practice that pays off generously.

Getting Into The Vortex: Guided Meditations CD and User Guide, by Abraham-Hicks: Has created a true masterpiece, which we have enjoyed since day one. "Getting into the vortex" means aligning with your highest self, which is also known as your direct connection to the divine, the broader part of who you are. The teachings of Abraham, in these guided meditations and book, refer to us as a direct extension of pure positive source energy, and that only a fraction of that becomes our physical form. It states that our purpose here is to live a life of contrast, recognizing that we don't want to recognize what we do want, in turn causing the Universe to expand. This practice is known as the Law of Attraction. The Law of Attraction states "The essence of that, which is like unto it, is drawn." In other words, you create your reality through your thoughts, both subconscious and conscious.

Don't Sweat the Small Stuff, and it's all small stuff by Richard Carlson, Ph.D.: List the perfect short read to help you realize the true significance of your conscious thoughts, and how a positive thinking perspective can change all of that.

This book shows you that you can calm down in the midst of any situation. Even in the incredibly hurried, stress-filled lives many people live in, this book will teach you how to put things in perspective by making small daily changes. One important quote that sticks out to us in this book is "Think of your problems as potential teachers." Worth the read, this book will definitely become a go-to guide in your reference list for positive thinking.

I hope that the above books help you in your journey, I have read a few of these and they have helped me. I hope you to have added them to your reading list. So that you can be the best version of yourself. There are many more books, out their go and discover some that you like.

Brain Games

There are games that you can use that help exercise your brain. Games like crosswords, Sudoku, and, reading books, all work to keeping your brain working. Others I like are Lumosity, Brain Games, Elevate, and Duo lingo, which is a language app. These are apps you can download to your phone or computer. I have used them for many years, now and I like how they are always creating new exercises. Mental exercises are important for keeping our brains working, like our muscles. Regular mental activities help our brains to stay in shape.

Your daily mental workout could start by having a glass of water, saying your affirmations, doing your exercise routine, playing some brain games as suggested above, reading for a half an hour, or what you mental exercise you like to do. Find out what gets you motivated and happy. Have a fun and positive day, every day.

Here are some suggestions on how to keep positive thoughts:

One chooses how to be positive. You can keep your thoughts positive, which makes you happy most of the time. For example, I like spending time with my wife, such as going out to a movie together. How great it is when you can say I love you!!

Of course, negative thoughts are there too. For example "I will never achieve this" negative thought. Or "I can't go to the gym; I am tired." These are negative thoughts. The more positive thoughts you have, the more you will be happy. Are you asking yourself how you can train your brain to think happy thoughts?

Have you noticed how some people feel bad about themselves when someone criticizes them, while others never seem to care? What most people don't know is that how you react to criticism is a habit, a thinking habit. You may be habitually taking it personally, and feel unhappy, while others are habitually indifferent, and keep on being happy. This can be true about everything you react to: how you react to compliments, how you react to bad drivers, how you react when you feel threatened or taken advantage of. By actively choosing different thoughts, you can reinforce the habit of thinking positively, and decrease the habit of thinking negatively. But what about occasions that are indeed negative. Does this mean you should deny the truth and wear rose-coloured glasses. No you can think positive and still be realistic. If you equate thinking positively as wearing rose coloured glasses, that's not what I am suggesting.

You can take a negative thought and reframe it. Here is an example. "I am so unfit." This is a negative thought that brings up bad feelings. You can reframe it by saying. " I am so unfit, BUT I am now exercising and getting fitter every day!" What started out as a negative thought, got twisted into a positive thought. The result is that you are one step closer to happiness. You can see how using BUT can magically keep your thoughts realistic and make you happier. If you could just add a harmless BUT to every negative thought you produce, you could transform all negative thoughts to positive ones. Here are some more examples:

- "I feel like I will never lose weight" becomes, "I feel like I will never lose weight, but I know there are other people who used to be exactly like me, and they made it happen!"

- "I will never pay off this debt." becomes "I will never pay off this debt, but I could pay some of it, if I start paying extra on it each pay check, by following my new budget plan."

The more you get used to adding *but* the better results you get, and the happier you will feel. At first, you will need to practice adding *but* to your negative thoughts. It may not feel natural when you first start out; however, the more you do it, the more your brain creates neural pathways that build the habit of automatically thinking with the word "BUT" every time you think negatively. The BUT technique will change the structure of your brain, and dramatically elevate you to a positive level. Being positive can be that easy.

Excellent!!!!

Affirmations

What are affirmations? They are words or quotes that have meaning to you, which will help keep you positive, successful, and on the path to a positive lifestyle.

Many people make meaningless affirmations. Have you noticed that your thoughts quickly jump from a positive thought to a negative thought? How about going directly to a positive thought each time? Are you wondering how to do that? The way you can do that is by using affirmations. The best way that works is to believe you can do it. For example, if you think, "I am so unfit, but now I am exercising and getting fitter every day," and if you are not very sure of your affirmation, then it makes it harder to make it a belief that will make a powerful thought. The BUT technique works marvellously; it accepts where you are, and shows you the road ahead. Identify your negative thought that you can turn into a positive one, with the simple use of the word BUT, now. Today is the day you can start training your brain to be positive.

Some other ways you can use affirmations are to find inspiring quotes online, or create your own. Copy them on to pieces of paper, or print them off. You can then leave the affirmations in different spots around your house, such as beside the bed, on the fridge, by the mirror in the bathroom, by the front door, on your phone's home screen, and other spots. You can even have a list that you read at night before bed, and in the morning when you get up. It's best to place them in locations that you see the most. Also, change them often so that your brain will be actively looking at them and not become blind to them over time.

By continually flooding your subconscious with positive thoughts and images, you will create a new reality.

Here is guideline to create positive affirmations:

- Start with the words "I am."
- Use the present tense.
- State it in the positive.
- Affirm what you want, not what you don't want.
- Keep it brief and make it specific.
- Include an action word ending with -ing.
- Include at least one dynamic emotion or feeling word.
- Make affirmations for yourself, not for others.

Here are some examples:

- "I am joyfully driving my new blue Tesla down the HOV lane on the QEW in Oakville"
- "I am so happy and grateful that I am earning $150,000 a year"
- "I am attracting joy into my life"
- " I am confidently expressing myself openly and honestly"
- "I am effectively communicating my needs and desires to my loving partner"
- "I believe in my skills and abilities"
- "I give myself space to grow and learn"
- "I listen to my intuition and trust my inner guide"
- "I give myself the care and attention that I deserve"
- "I trust myself to make the right decisions"

Make sure to take 5 to 10 minutes every day to repeat your affirmations. The best times are when you first get up in the morning and just before you go to bed. Make sure you use lots of positive energy and enthusiasm, when saying your affirmations!!!

Desserts

Dessert? What's that? You are thinking... it is the rewards we receive when we keep our positive life on the right path. It's like when you are going for the gold and are getting it. Or when you run the race you have been practicing for and get first place. The rewards I have experienced since being on my positive life journey, have included a more loving and understanding relationship with my wife and daughter. I have been able to move my personal improvement level up, not letting the negativity of others get me down, and I have learned to be more comfortable with myself.

Have you found that it is difficult to be persistent with staying with a new habit? For example, you try a new exercise routine and seem to quit a few days or weeks later. Why does this happen? One reason why you could have struggled is because it is really hard to stay consistent when you don't see the immediate results from your behavior change. Thankfully, there is a simple way to stick with your habits, goals, and tasks. Reward yourself whenever you hit an important milestone or achieve a specific goal. What is the logic in this? By having something to look forward to makes it easier to stick with a habit, especially when you're feeling a lack of motivation or are too tired to get started. Any reward you choose shouldn't derail your goals or habits. For example, if you are focusing on weight loss, and you achieve a breakthrough, don't pick a food reward, because that completely defeats the purpose of your accomplishment. Keep this in mind when you are setting rewards for yourself. Here are some ideas for rewards:

- Entertainment Rewards: Enjoy a laugh at a local comedy club, Go to a concert, go to an art gallery, marathon you favorite show on Netflix.

- Food Rewards: Enjoy a green superfood drink in the morning; buy your favorite pastry or cake, eat at your favorite restaurant; enjoy lunch outdoors, and cook your favorite dish. Using all those expensive ingredients.

- Free rewards: Call or spend a day with a friend or family member who makes you smile; color (get free adult coloring pages online); dance and sing; do some gardening; go *screen less* for a few hours; lie in a hammock; visit the library or bookstore by yourself; volunteer at the local shelter. These are some great suggestions. Find some of your own ideas too. Enjoy a positive lifestyle!!

Journaling

I have mentioned journaling throughout this book. Would you like to know how to do it better? How about some prompts? There are different types of journaling, but the one we are going to focus on is personal development!

What is difference between a traditional journal and self-improvement journal? The traditional journal has to do with external things. What you and other people said and did, or events that happened. The personal development journal is all about change. Getting from one place to another, a better place in your life and with yourself. You could do this type of journal daily or once a week.

What is the advantage of keeping a personal development journal? It helps recognize who you are today, where you want to go, how you plan on getting there, what you actually did to get there, and how that worked out. You could say they effect of this would be awareness or inducing consciousness. By recording these things you get an overview you wouldn't have had otherwise. This helps you learn and improve.

By keeping watch over the internal workings of your mind, you will bring your various mental processes into harmony with each other. Record your feelings, needs, actions, and beliefs. Evaluate everything and reflect on it. Then make decisions that will improve your life, and you will have a record of how they turned out.

Which way do you like to write? With pen and paper or computer? Here are some ideas about each.

If you love pen and paper:

You could just write on loose sheets of paper. This has the advantage of being something you can do anywhere and you can sort it out later, into folders or a ring binder. You should stick to one subject per page. If you want to write about a different subject, use a new piece of paper. You could get a blank journal that you could put index stickers in, to divide it for each subject you would like to improve on. A traditional diary works too.

If you love your computer:

Some people prefer writing on a computer, particularly those who use it a lot and who are, perhaps, much faster on a keyboard than with pen and paper. If you have a laptop or tablet, that's perfect, because you can make entries just about anywhere. You could use the word processor in your device. Start with writing a single document. Be sure to put dates for each entry and use headlines to make it easier to find info later. It's best to keep each document around 200 words, so it doesn't get too out of hand. Create a folder for your journal (PD journal) and have other subfolders for other subjects like money, relationships, career, spiritual, thoughts and ideas.

You could also use a dedicated diary app or calendar software for your personal development journal. You will need to learn how the app works, which should be easy. You should set it up following the method above.

Be sure that you can keep your information secure with both methods.

Make it password protected or store it on an external drive that is also password protected. Make sure you will remember you password.

What will you write about? You can write anything you want on your personal development. Here are some ideas that you can use in your personal development journal.

- Who you are
- How you like being that person
- Who you choose to be instead
- How you get to be the person you choose
- Where you failed and where you succeeded in your self-improvement
- What your life is like. How you like living that life
- Your past life experiences that you liked or didn't like
- Self-reflection and evaluation
- Wants, visions and goals
- Progress and results

These ideas should help you get started. Be total honest with your journaling. If you have secrets let them go, so your personal develop can excel.

What is the advantage of keeping a personal development journal?

- You can play with ideas, possibilities, wants, needs, dreams and visions. For example, you may want to eliminate a bad habit or switch to a more satisfying job. Great, not it in your journal; set a goal, consider what it takes and then start taking action.

- You can tell some really interesting and personal stories. You get a huge relief from being able to vent, by recording all your personal stuff, like what your greatest weaknesses and strengths are. It is like having a "shrink" for free. You will be able to notice habits and patterns plus evaluate and reflect on things you've never reflected on before.

- You can learn from your journaling. You learn a lot when you start recording your personal development initiatives, and the results from them, and start noticing your patterns and habits. Over time your will discover cycles in your life, and when you do, you can start to improve your life based on your new knowledge.

- You can improve your life in general and yourself as a person. Obviously this is the most important reason to keep a personal development journal. For example, in Canada during the winter it is often cold, and it gets dark earlier. This affects your mood and your outlook. By writing in your journal over the years, you will notice a pattern of negativity. You can then start to try out all sorts of things to change it, and become more positive during the winter season.

How do you use prompts to get you to start writing? Ask yourself, will this prompt be helpful? Is it to track progress/behavior/goals? To remember history? To stretch your mind?

Journaling should fun, helpful. Not a cause for stress.

Here is a list of prompts to help you:

- What are some places you've enjoyed visiting?
- What's a hobby you want to pursue?
- When did you last read a book, why did you read it, and what was it about?
- Write a food/movie review?
- What things are you grateful for?
- Would you consider being a minimalism?
- If someone wrote biography on you, what would the blurb be?
- If money where no object, how would you spend your time?
- What is your personal motto?

ABCs to a Positive Life

- What are your personal values?
- How are you a different person than you were years ago?
- Your five-year plan.
- How to manage your finances this year.
- If you could choose a mentor, who would it be?
- Your eulogy
- What person has been the strongest influence on you?

Chapter 4

An Appropriate Mindset

"If you have a positive attitude and constantly strive to give your best effort, eventually you will overcome your immediate problems and find you are ready for greater challenges".
Pat Riley

Setting the Stage

In order to get into the right mindset for the day, let's set our intentions when we first get up. Give yourself a big smile. Get up right away no snooze button. I used to be snooze button pusher. Then I started to leave my alarm clock on the other side of my bed, so I would have to get up to turn it off. This has worked wonders for me. These days I am able to get up without ever pushing the snooze button, even on weekends. To get yourself going, say an affirmation. "I am going to have a great day." Or "Success will come when I choose to feed my dreams and starve my doubts." Or I will read from my positive word list for inspiration. (Keep your list by your bed or alarm clock so that you can read it quickly after you wake you up.)

Also I will listen and watch a motivational video on You Tube, during my morning exercise time. These are simple activities that help me setting the stage for the day. Journaling helps me with getting ready for the day. When you do this in the morning, it will help set your goals or intentions for the day, week, or month.
You can also add a night time routine, which helps you be more

efficient in the morning. You can free up some time by being prepared the night before. For example, you can have your clothes laid out, and your breakfast ready to go. Your green smoothie or other health breakfast can be prepared. Your lunch can be ready. You can make your to do list for the day. You can also journal at night before bed, to help your subconscious improve your intentions. It can even help you get relief from your negative feelings and frustrations that have accumulated over the day. If they are still bothering you, this exercise will help you to deal with them. This can make your evening go smoother.

Once you have set up your positive morning and evening routine over time it will become second nature to you. You can create your own list. We each have different things that we need to get done. By starting your morning right and positive, it will make you a winner all day!!!!

The Right Way to Start the Day

Good morning to you and your big smiling face! It's all about you and how you decide to get going. As in the fine points above, like not hitting the snooze button, etc., we can add to the start of our work-day, with much of the same ideas. Each work day/ play day (plarking) day is different. So you can adjust your routine to how your positive mindset is going to be. In the beginning, it might be difficult some days, but you can adjust to your new attitude. Remember, it's yourself development and it's about you. Your decision to have a positive outlook helps you, and inspires others too.

Keep on winning throughout the day. Remember to write in your journal your gratitude and to-dos for the day. At the end of the day, review the day in your journal as well. If you have a negative situation, write it down, and find a solution to it. If you sleep on it, the solution may appear in your morning journal. These thoughts may take more work on your part to find the positive side.

Here is an inspiring story of Jim Carrey. When he was 14 years old, his father lost his job, and his family hit rough times. Thy moved into a VW van on a relative's lawn, and the young aspiring comedian, who was so dedicated to his craft that he had mailed his resumé to The Carroll Burnett Show just a few years earlier, took a pay-per-day factory job after school to help make ends meet.

At age 15, Carrey performed his comedy routine onstage for the first time, in a suit his mom had made him. He totally bombed, but he was undeterred. The next year, at 16, he quit school to focus on comedy full time. He moved to LA shortly after, where he would park on Mulholland Drive every night and visualize his success. One of these nights he wrote himself a check for $10,000,000 for acting services rendered, which he dated for Thanksgiving 1995. Just before that date, he hit his payday with Dumb and Dumber. He put the deteriorated check, which had kept in his wallet the whole time, in his father's casket.

Here is Oprah's story of inspiration. Oprah has dealt with a lot throughout her public life. Criticism about her weight, racism, intrusive questions about her sexuality, just to name a few. She never let it get in the way of her ambition and drive. When you look at her childhood, her personal triumphs are cast in an even more remarkable light. Growing up, Oprah was reportedly a victim of sexual abuse and was repeatedly molested by her cousin, an uncle and a family friend. Later she became pregnant and gave birth to a child at 14, who passed away just two weeks later. But Oprah persevered, going on to finish high school as an honors student, earning a full scholarship to college, and working her way up through the ranks of television, from a local network anchor in Nashville to an international superstar and creator of her OWN network.

The Right Environment

In order to make your life positive, you need the right environment. By this I mean that you should have other positive people and situations. Seek out others that are in tune with what you want. At first, it may be difficult. You might be surrounded by negativity but remember to make it a choice to be positive.

We can learn to deal with this by first recognizing it in others and our environments. The way I deal with it is to know that the other person has their own issues, and that they should not be affecting me. Also, be the better person and do not participate in their negativity. For example, if they are complaining don't make any comments on the conversation. It may be hard at first, but be mindful and don't get involved.

It's our choices that make our environment better for us. There are ways that can help you to get into a better environment. Join a team sport that you like, and that promotes a great team spirit. Have you tried to do some activities that you thought you would like to try? Mud run anyone? How about some rock climbing? How about something like doing a group vision board? Take a course on how to cook ethnic food of your choice. Join Toastmaster's group: they are great for helping you to be able to speak in public, and have some great leadership courses too.

If you have a family, you can make sure you set up your house to be more positive. You can create a positive atmosphere at home by making others feel safe, loved, heard, and respected. Your children will be affected by this environment for the rest of their lives and this will help them learn that they are good enough and deserve good things. They will be able to deal with difficulties in their lives better, and they will have the skills to guide them to be balanced, happy, and resilient. Be sure to use positive words and to reinforce good behaviours with praise. If they do something wrong, be sure to let them know that they are still loved after the fact.

Every moment you have a choice – to be at peace or to be in resistance. When you are at peace, you attract positive energy and when you resist you create negative vibes that reflect back on you. It is a choice you need to make. It's not your boss, colleagues, parents, ex or the traffic, but your own perception that creates stress and negative energy. Circumstances are neutral. You will generate positive vibes when your inner state is one of alignment and congruence, instead of being in resistance.

Here are some more points to help get you into your right environment.:

- Listen to uplifting music. The right music can heal and raise your vibrations. Create a playlist of songs that have a positive effect on you. Listen to this playlist every morning immediately after waking up or while getting ready for the day during your morning routine. Dance or move your body to the rhythm if you like. This way you can have some fun and shake off that morning lethargic energy from your body.

- Start your day with meditation. Any form of meditation is helpful, but it's best to keep it simple. Just practice the meditation of becoming aware of your presence. You can sit in a comfortable position, relax and feel your presence in the midst of your thoughts and emotions.

- Treat everyone the way you want to be treated. When you see others as yourself, you will not harbor negative feelings and in turn your attitude will attract positive energy form the people around you.

- Let go of your need to control. Whenever you try to control a life situation, you will feel stressed out and this will generate a lot of negative energy. Imagine life as a raging river; does it serve any purpose to struggle? Would it be more relaxing and peaceful if you just let go and allow yourself to go with the flow? People who stay relaxed generate a higher vibration and attract grace in their lives.

- Learn to see the positive in every situation. Know that good and bad are just perceptions created in the conditioned mind. In reality, every life situation is pure grace and is the manifestation of the one truth – call it good, spirit or universe. When you see every situation with innocence, it reveals its grace to you.

- Visualize a peaceful life. Your mind might be addicted to negative thinking. You will have to consciously break out of this addiction if you want to attract positive energy. Stay conscious and see your mind churning out fearful thoughts. Now, visualise a peaceful flow of life. Envision feeling calm and fulfilled. You will be amazed at the positive vibes you feel in your body.

- Stop worrying about the future. Worry has not served any purpose to anyone. What has to happen will happen; there is nothing you will achieve by worrying about it. In fact what you worry about will not even happen most of the time. So why waste energy dwelling on worries? By worrying you are unconsciously creating a lot of negative energy inside you, which is harmful to your whole being. Just plan practically and leave the rest to life.

End of Day Recall

So you made it through another successful day!!

Let's use our journals to write down the best parts or just some ides to improve our daily routine. It is always good to have a *mind dump* just to relieve ourselves of our daily stresses.

Some questions that you can ask yourself are:

- Did I choose to be positive today?
- How did I handle my self today?
- What magic power would I like to have?
- How would I use it?
- What would it feel like?
- What habits or routines should you start?

Here are some ideas:

- Make sure you get enough sleep each night. Your perfect amount is different from someone else. I am good with 7 hours a night. The amount varies by individual. What is your ideal sleep time? The way you feel while you're awake is dependent in part on your sleep habits. If you have been feeling foggy, irritable, or exhausted, you may not be getting enough quality sleep.

- During sleep, your body is working to support healthy brain function, and to maintain your physical health. In fact, sleep plays such a vital role in your physical well-being, mental clarity, and quality of life that ongoing sleep deficiency can have adverse effects on your health and how well you think, react, work, learn, and get along with others.

- Do you have a bed time routine? I like to have a camomile tea, read a book that is on my reading list, and write in my end of day journal. There are other ideas that you can do. Turn off your electronic screens. This includes phones, TVs, IPad, computers, Kindles, etc. If you are using your device for music, reading, or as an alarm/timer, set it on airplane mode and dim the screen light. Set up your sleep area so that it is quiet, dark, and warm/cool, so that you are physically comfortable. Reflect on your day/journal. Practice meditation. I like to use my muse head band to help me calm down before bed. However there are other ways to meditate. You can use your breath: inhaling for five seconds, hold for five seconds, and breathe out for five seconds. YouTube has lots of methods, find one that you like.

Here are some steps to create your best positive night routine:

- Accept that you are a great person. Go into your evening with and enthusiastic attitude to embrace the end of the day.

- Tidy up your space. It is great to wake up to a clean and organized space to help with your morning enthusiasm. Small things can make a big difference. Tidy your room, and clean the dishes and kitchen up the night before.

- Choose your clothes for the next day. Lay them out on your chair or hang them it up so that they are ready to jump into in the morning.

- Set goals for the next day. You should have three or four small goals for each day. Do the list before bed. This will help you to get the best out of your morning, and direct your focus. Also, your subconscious will help you while you sleep, to get them done more efficiently too. They can be as simple as a grocery list, or more complicated as to finishing your next book.

- Avoid multitasking. When you complete a task, focus all your energy on that job. Do not let your mind wander to the next item on your to-do list. If you feel your mind wandering, make a conscious effort to bring your focus back.

- Meditate. This activity will improve your evening. When you centre yourself, it will make your whole evening awesome.

- Budget your time. As you go through you evening routine, keep an eye on the clock. Give yourself a set amount of time to complete the basic tasks of getting ready. It is easy to lose track of time by lingering. You can set times for each part of your routine. For example spend 10 minutes on packing your lunch, 10 minutes on making your to-do list, etc. You decide on the time. If you find that you are not able to keep track, use your phone timer.

Once you have set up your positive morning and evening routine, over time it will become second nature to you. You can create your own list. We each have different things that we need to get done. By starting your morning right and positive, it will make you a winner all day!!!!

Recalling Your Best Moments of the Day, Week and Month

Hurray! You made it through another day, week and month. How do you think you did? What wins did you have? Who put a smile on your face? How did you deal with a negative person or situation? These are just some questions you can ask yourself as you go through recalling your day, week, and month.

- Remember that being positive is a choice.
- Get rid of negative people and situations.
- Look for the positive in everything.
- Reinforce positive thinking every time during the day.
- Share your positive attitude with others.

You should go through your journal at the end of the week to see what the good, the bad and maybe the ugly things were that have come up. What can you eliminate? If it is was good how do you make it better? What are some ways in which you can make someone else's day, week, or month better? Here are some ideas:

- Send thank you notes to people
- Pay for the person behind you in line at Tim Hortons or Starbucks
- Put a love note in your partner's or kids lunch
- Hold the door open for a stranger

- Surprise your spouse with lunch at work
- Tell someone they have a nice smile
- Have flowers delivered to your wife or mom, for no reason at all;
- Leave a more-than-generous tip for your server
- Say hi to a stranger
- Leave a beer on a friend's porch with a friendly note and then doorbell dash
- Volunteer at a charity
- Leave a message on a public mirror which says, "You are awesome"
- Tell someone how they inspired you
- Be grateful when others do things for you
- Leave a funny joke on someone's answering machine
- Ask a neighbor if they need anything at the store since you are going there anyway
- Shovel your neighbor's driveway
- Change the ringtone on your spouse's phone to something funny or to a song you both love, and don't tell them.

I hope these have helped. By doing good and fun things for others, it makes everyone more positive!

Sweet!! I hope you were able to get into an appropriate mindset from reading this chapter. Now, let's get to Chapter 5 and work with others and keep positive!!

Chapter 5

Being Positive with Others

"A positive attitude causes a chain reaction of positive thoughts, events and outcomes. It is a catalyst and it sparks extraordinary results." Wade Boggs

In this chapter, you will learn how to clear your mind of negative thoughts, and replace those thoughts with positive ones and positive words. You will learn how to deal with negative people and situations, so that you can be a newer and better you.

Using Clearing Techniques

Ho' oponopono: Yes it's a difficult word to pronounce. It means *"to make right"* in the Hawaiian language. This translates to taking 100% responsibility for what you have attracted. It is a technical effect that will help to change your outlook, by clearing your subconscious mind of disbelief, and by healing any wounds. You are realigning your truth within yourself.

Another one is affirmations. You can do your own affirmations. Do them in the present, and repeat them at least three times a day. An example would be. " I am abundant and prosperous. I follow my dreams no matter what." So think of some that relate to you that are positive and in the present tense. You are awesome!!!

The 3-Step Process by Gil McCliff

Feeling what you want is natural and easy; you are already doing this in many ways. The emphasis of this practice is on focusing on starving what you don't want, by simply observing the characteristics of your emotions and, thereby, dis-identifying from being them.

Your habitual state of consciousness is the number one determinant of your personal circumstances. The quality of your consciousness in this moment is the primary determinant of your future. And what determines the quality of your consciousness is your degree of presence.

Check in 10x a day with the question "What am I feeling emotionally in my body right now?"

You can use a reminder app on your phone, an alarm on your phone, sticky notes placed in random places, or you can paint one fingernail different from the rest, wear your watch on the opposite arm or upside down, or put a Band-Aid on your finger. Every time this catches your attention ask yourself, "Emotionally, how do I feel in my body right now?"

If there is ANY kind of negativity, or simply a lower emotion than what you would like to be feeling, the fact is that you did not choose it. It's based on conditioned interpretation and is simply an old program running, and it's time to do the following 3 steps: (*If you are feeling what you would like to be feeling then start with step 2.)

1. Say these specific words – "There it is. That's not me. That's a program."
2. Observe it deeply: What physical and emotional sensations do you feel? Where do you feel them? Or simply say "I feel it (here). It feels like (this)." Realize who is doing this inquiring.

3. Say "Thank you for releasing that. I love you. I love you. I love you. - Thank you for no longer feeding the program. Thank you for dis-identifying from the program; thank you for catching yourself and no longer losing energy here." Say "thank you for whatever you want to say thank you for," and also say " I love you, I love you, and I love you!" (*If it's a feeling you do desire, then say, "Thank you for expressing this. I love you. I love you. I love you.")

There it is. That's not me. That's a program. I feel it here (location); it feels like this (characteristics). Thank you for releasing that (or, thank you for expressing this). I love you. I love you. I love you.

These steps are not for the purpose of getting rid of the negative feeling, i.e. resisting and therefore feeding what we don't want. That benefit may sometimes come with it, but this practice is more about implementing a new habit/program. So every time you observe the emotion, it's an opportunity to do this practice without judgment. It doesn't matter what emotion is there; what matters is that you simply observe it without giving it any meaning. When this becomes a habit, you will have successfully reprogrammed the unconscious perpetuation of the old reaction, with the automatic newly programmed conscious response.

It takes less than 30 seconds to do this practice. 30 seconds at 10x a day = 5 minutes

How many days will it take before this healthy response has become a new program for you?

Replace Your Thoughts with Positive Ones

This sounds easy, but it can be difficult when first starting. The way to do this is that every time a negative word or thought comes to your attention, you will immediately replace it with a positive word or a positive thought. So, let's say that your word is "dark." You would replace it with "light." Or "hell" you could replace it with "heaven." You get the idea. The reason this works is that you cannot have both negative and positive in the same space. So by saying positive words or having positive thoughts, it will eliminate the negative. This is a great tool to help you start to think of ways to be positive. The goal with this awareness and replacement process isn't to completely prevent negative thoughts from entering your mind. That just is not realistic. The idea is to improve your ability to reduce and manage the negativity in your mind. As you get familiar with this process, you may find that it gets easier over time. There is no magic wand to take away stress and problems in life, but you hold the key to your quality of life. Start with articulating and acknowledging thoughts that are weighing you down, ones that do not serve your purpose beyond keeping you stuck. Releasing statements, such as "I forgive myself for procrastinating" or "It's ok for me to be angry" shortcut self-bashing and free up emotional resources.

If you spend less time beating yourself up for procrastinating, you can redirect that energy into more manageable tasks. Give interrogative self-talk a try. Asking yourself questions rather than issuing commands is a more effective way to create change. It's as simple as tweaking the way you speak to yourself. When you catch your inner critic flinging accusations, think: How can I turn this statement into a question? Asking questions opens up exploration and possibility. Here are some examples:

- Am I willing to do what it takes?
- When have I done this before?
- What if (insert worst case scenario) happens?
- How can I...?

This type of self-inquiry powers up problem-solving areas of the brain helping you tap into your innate creativity. You're able to greet negative thoughts with curiosity instead of fear.

Focus on progress, not perfection. Using a positive affirmation like "I am wonderful and powerful" may backfire if you don't truly, deeply believe it at both a cognitive and emotional level. To effectively reframe your thinking, consider who you are becoming, focusing on your progress and the current track or path you're on.

You might re-work your self-talk to sound more like "I am a work in progress, and that's OK." It's pointing you in the direction of positive growth and is both realistic and achievable. Another example: telling yourself "Every moment I'm making an effort to be more conscious about how I spend my money" acknowledges the fact that you are evolving and that you have choice in creating a better financial future for yourself.

In the next point, we will go through positive words.

Using Positive Words

Using positive words will keep you on track. It is great to have a list of positive words. I will list some here. You can create your own list, so that the words will resonate with you. Please check out www.ThePositiveLifeBook.com for a printable version.

ABUNDANCE, ACCOUNTABILITY, ACCOMPLISHMENT
BENEVOLENT, BELOVED, BEST,
CHARITY, CONFIDENCE, CONSCIOUSNESS
DESERVINGNESS, DETERMINATION, DEVOTION
EMPATHY, ENTHUSIASM, EXCELLENCE
FANTASTIC, FEEL GOOD, FORGIVENESS
GENEROSITY, GIGGLING, GRACIOUSNESS
HAPPINESS, HONOR, HUMOR
IMAGINATION, INSPIRE, INVINCIBLE
JOYOUS, JOKE, JUSTICE
KINDNESS, KEEN, KNOWLEDGE
LAUGHING, LEARN, LOVELY

MASTERY, MINDFULNESS, MODESTY
NICE, NIRVANA, NOURISH
OPTIMIST, OUTSTANDING, OPPORTUNITY
POSITIVE MIND, POLITE, PROACTIVE
QUALITY, QUIET, QUIESCENT
RESPONSIBILITY, RIGHTEOUSNESS, RELAX
SMILE, SELF-ESTEEM, SERVICE
THANKFULNESS, TRIUMPH, THRIVE
UPLIFT, UNDERSTAND, USEFUL
VICTORIOUS, VARIETY, VULNERABILITY
WORTH, WEALTH, WOW, WINNING
XO, X-RAY VISION, XFACTOR
YOUTHFUL, YES, YIPPEE
ZESTFUL, ZIPPY, ZANY

Dealing with Negative People

Dealing with negative people is a challenge, as I am sure you know. Some of the ways that can help are as follows:

- ignoring/ avoiding them
- replacing what they say to you with positive words. Find a way to rephrase what they say to a positive way, use an attitude of gratitude.

So you're wondering how to use these. Ignoring and avoiding is OK sometimes, but it can become an issue if you do it too often.

Replacing or rephrasing works because you can find a positive in what they are saying. Also, you can use your positive word list to keep your mind/mood in an upbeat state.

Gratitude works the best because you are giving thanks, to yourself and by rephrasing the situation, it becomes positive for you. Keep up the great work!!

ABCs to a Positive Life

Here are 9 tips to help you deal with negative people:

- Don't get into an argument. A negative person likely has very bad views and isn't going to change that just because of what you say. Whatever you say, he/she can find ten different reasons to back up his/her viewpoint. The discussion will just swirl into more negativity, and pull you down in the process. You can give constructive comments, and if the person rebuts with no signs of backing down, don't engage further.

- Empathize with them. Have you ever been annoyed by something before, then have someone tell you to "relax"? How did you feel? Did you relax as the person suggested or did you feel even more worked up? I have found that if you give an empathic ear, suggestion/solutions on what to do will benefit them more. By helping them to address their emotions, the solutions will automatically come to them.

- Lend a helping hand. Some people complain as a way of crying for help. They may not be conscious of it though, so their comments come across as complaints rather than requests. Take the onus to lend a helping hand. Just a simple "Are you okay?" or "Is there anything I can do to help?" can do wonders.

- Stick to light topics. Some negative people are triggered by certain topics. Take for example: One of my friends sinks into a self-victimizing mode whenever we talk about his work. No matter what I say (or don't say), he'll keep complaining when we talk about work. Some light topics could be new movies, daily occurrences, or common friends. Keep it to areas the person feels positive towards.

- Ignore the negative comments. One way to help the negative person "get it" is to ignore the negative comments. If he/she goes into a negative swirl, ignore or give a simple "I see" or "OK" reply.

On the other hand, when he/she is being positive, reply in affirmation and enthusiasm. Do this often and soon he/she will know that positivity pays off.

- Praise the person for the positive things. Negative people aren't just negative to others. They're also negative to themselves. If you already feel negative around them, imagine how they must feel all the time. What are the things the person is good at? What do you like about the person? Recognize the positive things and praise them for it. They will be surprised at first and might reject the compliment, but on the inside they will feel positive about it. That's the first seed of positivity you're planting in them, and it'll bloom in the long-term.

- Hang out in groups of 3 or more. Having someone else in the conversation works wonders in easing the load. In a one to one communication, all the negativity will be directed towards you. With someone else in the conversation, you don't have to bear the full brunt of the negativity. This way you can focus more on empathizing and helping the person.

- Be responsible for your reaction. Whether the person is negative or positive, ultimately you're the one who perceives the person's action. When you recognize that, the negativity is the product of your lens. Take responsibility for your perceptions. For every trait, you can interpret it in a positive and a negative manner. Learn to see the goodness of the person rather than the negative. It may be difficult in the beginning, but once you cultivate the skill, it becomes second nature.

- Reduce contact with them/avoid them. If all else fails, reduce contact with them or avoid them altogether. If it's a good friend let them know of the severity of the issue and work it out where possible. It's not healthy to spend too much time with people who drain you. Your time is precious, so spend it with people who have positive effects on you.

How to Be the New You

Now that you have been doing all of the positive practices, how do you feel? Have you noticed that things have been starting to change around you? Do you feel more confidence in yourself?

I hope that you are doing the best you can. I know I have been able to change my life by using these practices. Most days are great, and some are OK. I know that I have the power to change how I feel and react to my environment.

Being consistent and persistent will keep your positive life on the winning side!

Here is a story:

Once upon a time a psychology professor walked around on a stage while teaching stress management principles to an auditorium filled with students. As she raised a glass of water, everyone expected they'd be asked the typical "glass half empty or glass half full" question. Instead with a smile on her face, the professor asked, "How heavy is this glass of water I'm holding?"

Students shouted out answers ranging from eight ounces to a couple of pounds. She replied, "From my perspective, the absolute weight of this glass doesn't matter. It all depends on how long I hold it. If I hold if for a minute or two, it's fairly light. If I hold it for an hour straight, my arm will likely cramp up and feel completely numb and paralyzed, forcing me to drop the glass to the floor. In each case, the weight of the glass doesn't change, but the longer I hold it, the heavier it feels to me.

As the class shook their heads in agreement, she continued, "Your stresses and worries in life are much like this glass of water. Think about them for a while and nothing happens. Think about them a bit longer and you begin to ache a little. Thing about them all day long and you will feel completely numb and paralyzed. Incapable of doing anything else until you drop them."

The moral: It's important to remember to let go of your stresses and worries. No matter what happens during the day, as early in the evening as you can, put all your burdens down. Don't carry them through the night and into the next day with you. If you still feel the weight of yesterday's stress, it's a strong sign that it is time to put the glass down.

Chapter 6

Your Why to a Positive Life

"Choosing to be positive and having a grateful attitude is going to determine how you're going to live your life."
Joel Osteen

Welcome to Chapter 6. In this chapter, we will find your *why to a positive life*, and which people to look up to. We will learn how to use self-hypnosis to strengthen your mindset and to choose your own affirmations.

Discovering Your Positive Lifestyle

Now that you have done some clearing exercises, and have discovered some of your positive traits, let's start to put the parts together.

Write down a list of 20 things that you like about yourself, and that you think you are good at. Think of things you have done, such as - giving money to charity, helping someone cross the street, or giving someone a smile, all of these things count.

Have you started a gratitude journal? It it's a good time to start. You can write in it every day about all the things you are grateful for. It can be as simple as... *I am grateful for being awake early today.* I am grateful for a warm house. I am grateful for the food I enjoy and have in abundance.

Please create your own gratitude journal to keep yourself positive. Take responsibility. You can shape your future, but only if you learn to be brave and take risks. Positive people take risks, even if they are scared.

Developing a positive lifestyle has more to do with how you choose to perceive situations than about the situations themselves. No one can feel positive all the time, and it is debatable whether that would be a good idea anyway. After all, our appreciation of what we have tends to be greater when we have had to strive to get or keep it. Just make it a habit.

Eat more healthy food and less junk food. Exercise your body regularly. You can walk, swim, run, go to the gym, or do any sport you like. I like mud runs, and working out at the gym.

Resist the temptation to procrastinate and postpone for tomorrow or to an indefinite date, what you can do today. The Universe likes speed and action.

Remember, if you want to live a positive lifestyle, you need to take control of your life. You need to be proactive with your life, not passive. Do not just daydream and wish things were different. Do not wait for a better and happier day. Get out there and get it done today! Seeks out the good, and make your day beautiful, even if there are dark clouds. Expect the best, but also do your best. Be the one who decides, and make your life better and happier.

A great and most helpful tool for adopting a positive lifestyle is the habit of repeating affirmations. It is a simple and easy to use tool - remember your list of positive words? Remember the affirmations that were in Chapter 3? These will help in writing your affirmations in a more positive style.

Whom to Look Up To

Who are your heroes? Is there someone that has made a positive impact on your life?

There are lots of motivational speakers. I like Les Brown, Bob Proctor, and Raymond Aaron.

For me, these people have influence my life in many ways. Watching them on stage, or listening to their audios on various topics, has encouraged me to be better and to live my own positive life.

I have found that listening to the audios respectively has had the greatest impact, because it gets into my subconscious mind, there by changing my programming and influencing my conscious mind.

A mentor or a coach will help you with your journey. Here are 5 reasons to have a mentor:

1. They've been there and done that. You can learn from your mentor's mistakes, and avoid making them yourself.
2. You can talk to someone who is an unbiased third party. They see you for you. Your mentor may notice potential in you that you might not see in yourself. Better yet, they are not your boss, so you don't have to worry about things coming up in your review. And they are not your parents, so you can actually listen to them!
3. They have a whole different network of contacts and connections that you don't have. These connections are priceless and can help enhance your career in ways you couldn't yourself.
4. It's the best free service you could ever get. AND you'll probably gain a life-long friend.
5. Your mentor may introduce you to a career path or business opportunity that you did not know existed before.

Using Self-Hypnosis to Increase Your Mindset

How can I use self-hypnosis to achieve my goals?

Self-hypnosis is often used to modify behavior, emotions and attitudes. For instance, many people use self-hypnosis to help deal with the problems of everyday living. Self-hypnosis can boost confidence and even help people develop new skills. A great stress and anxiety reliever, it can also be used to help overcome habits such as smoking and overeating. Sports men and women can enhance their athletic performance with self-hypnosis, and people suffering from physical pain or stress-related illnesses also find it helpful (Hypnosis should only be used in this way after a medical diagnosis has been made, and under the guidance of a doctor or qualified therapist.)

A self-hypnosis technique

A simple but effective technique of self-hypnosis is eye fixation self-hypnosis, and it is one of the most popular and effective forms of self-hypnosis ever developed. We will start by using it as a method to help you relax. After you have practised this a number of times, we will add hypnotic suggestions and imagery. To start, reduce distractions by going into a room where you are unlikely to be disturbed, and turn off your phone, television, computer, etc. This is your time. You are going to focus on your goal of self-hypnosis, and nothing else. You should set a timer for 5 minutes, and have the alarm start low and rise to a louder volume. Then:

1. Sit in a comfortable chair with your legs and feet uncrossed.

    Avoid eating a large meal just before, so that you don't feel bloated or uncomfortable. Unless you wish to nod off, sit in a chair, as lying down on a bed will likely induce sleep. You may also wish to loosen tight clothing and take off your shoes. If you wear contact lenses, it is advisable to remove them. Keep your legs and feet uncrossed.

2. Look up at the ceiling, and take in a deep breath.

   Without straining your neck or tilting your head too far back, pick a point on the ceiling and fix your gaze on that point. While you keep your eyes fixed on that point, take in a deep breath and hold it for about 5 seconds, and then breathe out. Silently repeat the suggestion, "My eyes are tired and heavy, and I want to SLEEP NOW," or another positive mantra if you like. Repeat this process to yourself another couple of times and, if your eyes have not already done so, let them close and relax in a normal closed position. It is important when saying the suggestion that you say it to yourself as if you mean it, in a gentle, soothing but convincing manner.

3. Let your body relax.

   Allow your body to become loose and limp in the chair, just like a rag doll. Then, slowly and with intention, count down silently from five to zero. Tell yourself that with each and every count, you're becoming more and more relaxed. Stay in this relaxed state for a number of minutes while focusing on your breathing. Notice the rising and falling of your diaphragm and chest. Be aware of how relaxed your body is becoming without you even having to try and relax it. In fact, the less you try, the more relaxed you become.

4. When ready, come back to the room by counting up from one to five.

   Tell yourself that you are becoming aware of your surroundings, and at the count of five, you will open your eyes. Count up from one to five in a lively, energetic manner. At the count of five, open your eyes and stretch your arms and legs.

Repeat this technique three or four times, and notice how each time you reach a deeper level of relaxation. However, if you find that you do not relax as much as you would like, do not force it. There is a learning curve involved, so resolve to practice self-hypnosis on a regular basis.

Sometimes people will feel a little spaced out or drowsy after they come out of the hypnosis. This is similar to awakening from an afternoon nap; it is harmless, and it passes after a few moments. However, do not drive or operate machinery until you feel fully awake.

Difficulties learning self-hypnosis

Have you ever experienced the frustration of having a name on the tip of your tongue? The harder you try to remember the name, the harder it is to recall. Then, when you relax, the name comes back to you. Sometimes, when we try too hard, we block ourselves from achieving our goals. The attitude you take towards self-hypnosis will determine how easily you learn it. Don't try too hard or set unrealistic goals. Relax and take your time. Accept the pace at which you achieve results, however slow it may at first seem. Believe in yourself, and you will go on to achieve the success you desire.

Post-hypnotic suggestions and their rules

As previously mentioned, hypnosis is a state of heightened suggestibility. Giving you suggestions when in hypnosis will enable an action or other responses to take place after the hypnotic experience has occurred. These forms of suggestion are called post-hypnotic suggestions, and will help you to achieve your goals. Over the years, hypnotherapists have developed rules of suggestion. These are guidelines that will enable you to achieve maximum success with the suggestions you give yourself. What follows is a summary of these rules.

ABCs to a Positive Life

1. Say it as if you mean it.

   Have you ever seen an actor mumbling his lines on stage, speaking in a quiet, meek voice? The result is a performance that's not very convincing. Unlike acting, hypnotic suggestions are repeated silently. However, you need to repeat the suggestions as though you mean what you say. Be reassuring, positive, and confident.

2. Suggestions need to be phrased positively and in the present tense.

   Most of us will react more favourably to a positively worded suggestion than to a negative one.

   Which request would you rather hear: "Do not leave that lying on the floor?" or "Would you mind picking that up?"

   Suggestions are far more effective when you mention what you wish to move toward, rather than what you are moving away from. For example, "I am calm," is better than "I am not anxious," "I stop smoking with ease," is better than, "I will try to stop smoking," as the word *try*, implies difficulty and struggle.

   Your suggestions are best phrased in the present tense, as though they are happening at this moment in time.

   So, "I am relaxed on the aircraft" is better than, "I will be relaxed when I am on the aircraft," Or, "I am becoming more confident," is better than "I will try to be confident."

3. Make your suggestions specific and realistic.

   Your suggestions are going to be more effective if they are specific and realistic. If you wish to improve your swimming performance, it would be unrealistic to give yourself the suggestion, "I am a world-class swimmer," unless of course you are, or are about to become, a world champion. Instead, ask yourself what specifically it is about your swimming that you wish to improve. So, if you wish to improve your breaststroke, you would give yourself a realistic suggestion tailored to that specific aspect of your swimming. Structure your suggestions on changes you wish to see in yourself, rather than on things that are out of your control, such as external events and other people. Do not give yourself suggestions for two or three issues all at the same time. For instance, the suggestion "I am confident that I can lose weight and stop smoking," is probably not effective. Instead, work on one goal at a time, repeating suggestions associated with that goal. When you see some results, move on to your next goal.

4. Repetition of suggestions

Advertisers know the value of suggestion, which is why they repeat television and radio commercials on a regular basis. One of the most important rules, when practising self-hypnosis, is repetition of your suggestions. That way, you drive the point home and are far more likely to affect positive change.

Imagery in hypnosis

While giving yourself hypnotic suggestions, visualise the situation, the action and the feeling that you desire. As well as picturing a desired outcome, you can utilise your sense of touch, hearing, and even smell. You can create new images as well as using images from your memories and experiences. People sometimes believe they have to see a crystal clear image of their goal, as though watching a movie. However, a positive attitude and a belief that you are "in the role" is more important than clear imagery.

The following exercise will illustrate how effective suggestion and imagery can be. Do not use it if you have an aversion to lemons.

- Sit down in a comfortable chair and close your eyes.
- Picture an ordinary lemon.
- Imagine you are cutting this lemon in half.
- Observe the juices running down each piece of the lemon.
- Pick up a piece of the lemon. Bring it up to your mouth and bite into it.
- Even if your image of the lemon wasn't clear, you might still have grimaced, or even found your mouth watering.

As you can see, using imagery helps bring your suggestions in to reality.

There are also You Tube videos and other information online if you would like to explore this more. I use You Tube for my night time meditation. It helps me get a better sleep and I feel great in the morning.

Please check out www.positivelifebook.com for videos I uploaded I like and use.

Writing Your Own Affirmations

As in one of the previous chapters, I mentioned affirmations. In this point, we will work on our own affirmations. Some questions we can ask ourselves are....

What is my goal? What are my negative thoughts? How can I make them positive? Now that we have asked ourselves some questions, let's go through some basic affirmation writing steps.

1. Write out affirmations that are on the positive side of your negative beliefs of yourself. An example would be to change "I am not worthy;" to "I am worthy." Or even better, "I am remarkable and cherished."
2. Write in the present tense. Your writing should be as though you are experiencing it right now.
3. Reflect deep kindness to yourself.
4. Make it personal. *Use words like. I, my or state your name in your affirmations.* This will deepen the belief level.
5. Go easy on the amount of affirmations you write. Aiming for good quality affirmations that haves a profound impact on you is more valuable.

These are some easy steps that will help you. So, let's get some affirmations down on paper, and start posting them around your house or office. Also, say them out loud, and repeat them 4 times every day - once in the morning, at lunch, at dinner, and before you go to bed. The repetition will deepen the belief and help your subconscious to be reprogrammed so that it will become automatic for you in the future.

Here are some affirmations:

- I am a magnet for abundance and success.
- I am an accomplished and successful person.
- Everything is happening perfectly in my life.
- I attract wealth into my life.
- I attract love into my life.
- I love myself.
- My life is fun and filled with joy.
- I am smart and make good choices.
- I can overcome any obstacle.

Here are some of the affirmations I use:

- Success will come when I chose to feed my dreams and starve my doubts.
- I am a multi-millionaire.
- I am a money magnet.
- Every day, and in every way, I am getting better and better.
- Gratitude is the single most important ingredient to living a successful and fulfilled life.

This is my mission statement: My personal mission is to develop and cultivate the qualities of loyalty, commitment, a positive attitude, and consistence. The person I admire is Raymond Aaron, so that I can be a person of value to others, and to be of greatness in the world today, and make millions of people happy through my book, *ABCs to a Positive Life*.

My vision statement: To become a New York Times bestselling author. To be a multi-millionaire, to be a fantastic coach, speaker, author, philanthropist, so that I can help others to achieve their best life. To do more activities, adventures and traveling with my family. I will do this by generating multiple streams of income by writing more books, having a thriving coaching and speaking business, and becoming an affiliate with multiple companies. I will continue to learn by reading books, going to seminars, workshops and masterminds.

The One Thing That Has Made You Change

Have you found your, why to your positive life? Or a better question is, what can you do with your time, which is important? This is the power to your *why*.

Also, what level of failure are you willing to tolerate to get to your desired goal? If someone had put a gun to your head, what would you do to get to your goal? If you knew you were going to die one year from today, what would you do, and how would you want to be remembered? What is your legacy going to be? What are the stories people are going to tell when you are gone?

Discovering your *why* in life essentially boils down to finding those one or two things that are bigger than yourself, and bigger than those around you. It's not about some great achievement, but merely finding a way to spend your limited amount of time well. Also, you must get off your couch and act, and take the time to think beyond yourself, to think greater than you, and paradoxically, to imagine a world without you.

How do you find your why? Here are some suggestions: Block out some *me time*, and put a lot of thought into this. What is your why? You can flip through magazines and see what appeals to you. You can make a vision board, which can help reveal some deep desires. Do some soul searching, and get serious in your thinking. Ask yourself some questions: Do you want to be healthy? To feel great daily? To be around and active for your children? To make more money?

There is no wrong "why." It just needs to have great meaning and be personal to you! Also, you can't use somebody else's why, and just make it yours. It does not matter what others think. You have to make it important to you. Once you get to the root of what your why is, it changes and drives you. All of a sudden, solutions will start presenting themselves to your problems. The hurdles become crystal clear, and you start to take action and make things happen all because you found out what drives you. You found your *why*. Discovering your WHY is the most important step to changing, as it gets your mind right. When your mind is active and focused on positive things, you will get positive results.

I hope these questions you have answered have helped you find your reason to be better with your positive life.

Chapter 7

The Right Way to Self-Talk

"Do not wait; the time will never be 'just right.' Start where you stand, and work with whatever tools you may have at your command, and better tools will be found as you go along."
George Herbert

Yes, chapter 7! In this chapter, we will be going through how to keep your personal self-talk positive, as well as being optimistic, having self-confidence, and doing more affirmations. Let's get to work!!!

Keeping the Self-Talk Positive

This is important for keeping yourselves on the path of positive life. Positive self-talk develops a positive attitude. So, whenever you realize that you are having negative self-talk, try these steps to overcome it.

1. Say "STOP" to yourself.
2. Close your eyes and take a deep breath.
3. Hold your breath for eight seconds and breathe out for eight seconds.
4. During this time try to change you negative talk to successful, positive self-talk.
5. Create a feeling of success, and say the positive self-talk to yourself again, out loud.

An example would be, when you telling your inner voice is saying "I cannot do this," change it to "let's see what I can learn when I give this a try." Or change, "No one even cares enough to know my name" to "This is an opportunity to make a good impression on them."

Also, create a healthier environment. Start to surround yourself with positive people. This will help to embrace your own positivity, and make it easier to change yourself.

Since I have started to go to seminars, workshops, and meetings, with people who are also looking to be better and improve themselves, I have found that my attitude has changed. I have a more positive outlook. My self-esteem has gone way up. I feel that I can do it. Also, my knowledge of my life and my business ideas has increased. It's GREAT!!! I also eat healthy by following a clean diet and I exercise regularly. This has also helped to keep my stress levels low, because a healthy body supports healthy mental and emotional states.

Affirmations

There are different types of affirmations. Here is a list of the types:

Today I believe

- I am a person with a lot to offer.
- I will make a difference in someone else's life.
- I can contribute positively at work.
- I am beautiful. I love my eyes/nice smile/strength/great shirt/etc.
- I am a good friend.
- I am a great listener.
- I am creative.
- I have a purpose in life; I have worth.
- I don't need to avoid interacting with others, because I like myself.
- I will look people in the eye.
- I don't need to compare myself to others.

- I will do my best and that will be enough.
- I am okay with not being perfect, no one is.
- I am capable of seeing beauty in the world, and knowing that I am a part of it.
- I realize that my small mistakes don't reflect my whole self or experience.
- I will make the most out of life, and love myself!

Examples of self-love and self-esteem

- I am the creator of my life at every moment.
- I open myself to the beauty of life.
- I open myself to my own beauty.
- I face the challenges of my life.

Examples of powerful affirmations for work

- I love my job.
- I am rewarded for my good work.
- I am well prepared for my job.
- I am appreciated my customers.

Examples of powerful affirmations for love

- I am attractive.
- I love my partner.
- I am loved by my partner.
- I am valued by my partner.
- I love with all of my heart.

Examples of powerful affirmation for weight loss

- I love my body.
- I lead a vital life.
- I accept my appearance and my body.

- I feel physically strong.
- I am full of love, hope and self-confidence.

Examples of powerful affirmations for attitude of gratitude

- I have an attitude of gratitude.
- My thoughts are focused on positivity and thankfulness.
- I am sincerely grateful and this attracts positivity into my life.
- I am grateful for my family.
- I am thankful for simply being alive.

Examples of positive law of attraction affirmations

- The law of attractions works.
- I use positive thinking and beliefs to manifest a positive life
- I have the power to create my reality.
- I believe in the law of attraction.
- I believe deeply that I can achieve anything I desire.

Find ones that work for you. Once you have a list written out, record those with your phone so you can listen to them repetitively during your morning routine, on your drive to work or even while you brush your teeth. This will deepen the affirmation into your subconscious, and will become more and more believable to your conscious mind.

Check out www.thepositivelifebook.com for a printable version

Ho Oponopono

This method works wonders. I have used it during my drive home. The best example is when someone cuts me off. Normally, I would get mad or curse. Now I use Ho Oponopono and it makes the drive home more enjoyable. Just by saying these words... I love you. I am sorry. Please forgive me. Thank you. I love you. I am sorry. Please forgive me. Thank you....

ABCs to a Positive Life

By using these words when I am mad or have a negative feeling, it helps me to feel love, and my feelings or emotions begin to transform to positive ones. By doing this consistently, it helps to reprogram my subconscious, and then my automatic reactions will be positive ones, which makes me happier and maintain an abundance of positivity. Also, I have found that even if I just use some of the Ho opono pono saying it will still help me remove my negativity, and automatically, things will be better. It is best to do this regularly throughout the day, even when things are going well. It will also help others around you feel better, and your outcomes will be more positive as well. Ho Oponopono is the Hawaiian system that heals oneself and the world too.

Here is some history on Ho Oponopono:

More than thirty years ago, in Hawaii, at the Hawaii State Hospital, there was a special ward: a clinic for the mentally ill criminals. People who had committed extremely serious crimes were assigned there, either because they had a very deep mental disorder, or because they needed to be checked to see if they were sane enough to stand trial. They had committed serious crimes.

According to one nurse that worked there in those years, the place was so bleak that not even the paint could stick to the walls; everything was decaying, and it was terrifying, and repulsive. Not a day would pass without a patient/inmate attacking another inmate or a member of the staff. The people working there were so frightened that they would walk close to the walls if they saw an inmate coming their way in a corridor. Even though they were shackled, all the time, this wouldn't stop their aggression. The inmates could never be taken outside to get fresh air, because of their relentless threatening attitude. The scarcity of staff was a chronic occurrence. Nurses, wardens, and employees would prefer to be on sick-leave most of the time in order not to confront such a depressive and dangerous environment.

One day, a newly appointed clinical psychogist, Dr. Stanley Hew Len, arrived at the ward. (Dr. Hew Len was the teacher of the healing system, Ho Oponopono.) The nurses rolled their eyes, bracing themselves for one more guy that would be bugging them with new theories and proposals to fix the horrid situation, who would walk away as soon as things became unpleasant, usually around a month later.

However, this new doctor wouldn't do anything like that. Actually, he didn't seem to be doing anything in particular, except just coming in and always being cheerful and smiling, in a very natural, relaxed way. He wasn't even particularly early in arriving every morning. From time to time, he would ask for the files of the inmates. He never tried to see them personally. Apparently, he just sat in an office and, looked at their files. For members of the staff who showed an interest, he would tell them about a weird thing called Ho Oponopono. Little by little, things started to change in the hospital. One day, somebody would try again to paint those walls, and they actually stayed painted, making the environment more palatable. The gardens started being taken care of, and some tennis courts were repaired. Some prisoners that up till then would never have been allowed to go outside, started playing tennis with the staff. Other prisoners would be allowed to be shackled any more, or would receive less heavy pharmacological drugs.

More and more prisoners obtained permission to go outside unshackled, without causing trouble to the hospital's employees. In the end, the atmosphere changed so much that the staff was not on sick leave any more. Actually, then more people wished to work there. Prisoners gradually stared to be released. Dr. Hew Len worked there for close to four years. In the end, there remained only a couple of inmates who were relocated somewhere else when the clinic for mentally insane criminals had to be closed.

Being Optimistic

Optimism is a mental attitude reflecting a belief or hope that the outcome of some specific endeavour, or outcomes in general, will be positive, favourable, and desirable. An optimist would see a glass as half full, whereas a pessimist would see it as half empty.

In my own life, my optimistic outlook helped me when my wife and I had our first baby...

On Father's Day my wife was complaining about a massive headache. We went home and she took some Advil. About 2am, she said she wanted to go to the hospital... this is where it got very scary. We were not sure what was going to happen, but we keep a positive outlook. Reta was rushed to Mac Master Hospital. That was when we found out that she needed to deliver the baby early. They were able to keep Reta and the baby in the hospital for another week. So at 27 weeks we had London. She was the most amazing baby, weighting in at 2lbs and 1oz.

For the next 3 months, I was at the hospital every day after working 12 - 14 hrs. I was so tired, but it was the most amazing feeling to see my daughter every day. The best part was kangaroo care, which was where my daughter would lie on my bare chest, just in her diaper, with half a dozen tubes and wires. The feeling was amazing, and we are able to connect, in a way I never knew or have felt before.

The reason why you do kangaroo care is that it is something special for your baby that only you can give. Kangaroo care helps the baby: maintain its body warmth, and regulate the heart and breathing rates. It helps the baby gain weight, spend more time in deep sleep (which happened for me too), and spend more time being quiet and alert with less time crying, as well as having emotional benefits. It built my confidence and reduced my stress, as I was providing intimate care that was improving my daughter's health and well-being.

On Father's day, in 2014, we were at my uncle's having Father's Day dinner with family. The house was crowded, so most of us were outside. Earlier, Reta was complaining that she had a head ache. My uncle is great at cooking on the BBQ. We had some great food, and I was actually full.

After dinner, Reta's headache got worse, so we decide to go home. I asked Reta if she thought we should go to the hospital to make sure everything was okay. She said she was okay and thought it was just part of pregnancy. The head ache got worse through the night. So, about 2am, Reta said that we needed to go to the hospital. We raced off to emergency. The staff at the hospital did their usual thing for registering, but we didn't wait long. Once the doctor saw Reta, they knew we had a problem. They called Mac Master to assist them in stabilizing Reta, as the hospital we first went to was not equipped to handle a premature birth. I was really worried because I did not know what was going on. The doctors stabilize Reta so that she could be transferred to Mc Master by ambulance. I drove to Mc Master and I was really worried at this time. Some of my thoughts were that we could lose the baby or that Reta wouldn't make it. But I kept a positive attitude; I knew we were in professional hands.

At first, we thought we would lose the baby because of all the pain my wife was in. That Father's Day was one I will never forget. Also, when I got to Mc Master I was not sure what was going on with Reta. It was only 1/2 hour, but it seemed like a life time. When I saw the nurse, and she said that Reta was stable, I was so relieved. Although it had been 3 months at the hospital, it didn't seem that long. Seeing my daughter every day changed my outlook. I felt that I need to be better, make more money, and be the best dad I can be.

This is where I am today. It took a few years, but I am heading in the right direction.

Self-Confidence

> *"Calm mind brings inner strength and self-confidence, so that's very important for good health."*
> Dalai Lama

Self-confident people are admired by others and inspire confidence in others. They face their fears head-on, and tend to be risk takers. They know that no matter what obstacles come their way, they have the ability to get past them. Self-confident people tend to see their lives in a positive light, even when things aren't going so well, and they are typically satisfied with and respect themselves.

Does this sound amazing, to have this level of self-confidence? You can with 5 simple steps:

1. Bring on the positive

   Be positive, even though you are not feeling it. Put some positive enthusiasm into your interactions with others. Focus on solutions, and make positive changes.

2. Change your body language and image.

   This is where posture, smiling, eye contact, and speech come into play. Just by pulling your shoulders back will give the impression that you are a confident person. Smiling will make you feel better, and will make those around you more comfortable too. Go the extra mile and style your hair; give yourself a good cleaning, and dress nicely. Not only will this make you feel better about yourself, but others are more likely to perceive you as successful and self-confident as well. A great tip: When you purchase a new outfit, practice wearing it at home first, to get past any wardrobe malfunctions before heading out.

3. Don't accept failure, and get rid of the negative voices in your head.

    Never give up. Never accept failure. There is a solution to everything, so why would you want to throw in the towel. Succeeding through great adversity is a huge confidence booster. Keep using your positive affirmations.

4. Be prepared.

    Learn everything that you can about your field, job, presentation, or what is next on your to-conquer list. When you are prepared and have the knowledge to back it up, your self-confidence will soar. Also, don't dwell too much on perfection here; it can be come overwhelming and lead in procrastination.

5. Create a great list.

    Sit down and make a list of all the things in your life that you are thankful for. Make another list of all the things you are proud of accomplishing. Once your lists are complete, post them on your refrigerator or on the wall by your desk, or on your bathroom mirror, where you can be reminded of what an amazing life you have and what an amazing person you really are. If at any time you feel your self-confidence dwindling, take a look at your lists, and let yourself be inspired again.

Chapter 8

Leading the Way

"Leadership and learning are indispensable to each other."
John F. Kennedy

Believe in Yourself

*"Believe in yourself, and the rest will fall into place.
Have faith in your own abilities, work hard and
there is nothing you cannot accomplish."*
Brad Henry

The basis of gaining a positive life is believing in you. *Believe in yourself!* Ultimately, you are the only person that can truly believe in yourself-nobody else can.

The next time you struggle with self-doubt or negative thinking, ask yourself this question:

How would the person I would like to be, do the same thing I am about to do? Then, simply be that person you would like to be, regardless of the doubts running through your mind.

Practice daily positive self-talk, cut the negativity from your life, and focus on the consistent small steps. Then you will be on your way to achieving your positive life. Much like eating a whole elephant, you need to do it one bit at a time.

Also, your self-image is part of believing in yourself. A good practice is as follows: Every morning, and every night before bed, set a timer to 3 minutes. Stand in front of a mirror and simply talk to yourself, using your positive words list and or your affirmations to counter act any self-doubts.

For example, tell yourself, "My work is unique and good enough to be shared with the world," instead of "My work is not good enough." Rinse and repeat for 30 days!!

Make sure you take care of yourself by taking a shower and brushing your teeth daily. Have a workout routine; it can be as easy as doing some stretching, and doing some push-ups, sit-ups, and some chin ups. Or even have a morning or evening walk and then work up to a run!

"If you spend an extra hour each day of study in your chosen field you will be a national expert in that field in 5 years or less."
Earl Nightingale

Here are 5 daily reminders to keep saying to yourself:

1. I am amazing
2. I can do anything
3. Positivity is a choice
4. I celebrate my individuality
5. I am prepared to succeed.

To have a better understanding of what it means to believe in yourself, you need to understand what it means to believe in someone else.

Some of the qualities I look for are whether, the person is trustworthy, and that he/she never lies; they always speaks the truth, always delivers what he/she promises, and they always walk the talk.

You should use the following qualities. Behave in a trustworthy manner to yourself and to others. To maintain this, I would say that you would need knowledge of yourself, knowledge of people, knowledge of reality, a vision of your future, an ability to make the right decisions, the courage to follow your convictions, an ability to with-stand pressure, an ability to resist temptation, a sound strategy to achieve your objectives, you should remain honest even when no one is watching.

Getting Out of Your Way

Getting out of your own way means being with whom you are, moment to moment, whether you like it or not, and whether or not it is easy or comfortable, familiar or disturbing, and then creating from that place.

There will always be a reason why you should or should not do something. The trick... you just start, push through any insecurity that is stopping you. Once you start, momentum will keep you rolling past any obstacles. So pull the trigger NOW!!!

How many times have you multi-tasked? Did you get more things done? I know that I don't. I have started things and then left them. So, like juggling, I have too many things up in the air, and suddenly, I miss a step and drop everything. A better way would be to focus on one thing at a time and then move on to the next. Like the domino effect, knock one down, and then one at a time the others fall too.

Forget failure; it will happen, and is a necessary part of the process. Do your best to learn from it, and move on. Be consistent. Unfailing hard work will help maintain the momentum, which will become a good habit. Next, make sure you are hanging with the right people. They directly influence who you are and what you do. Make sure you surround yourself with people who encourage you and hold you accountable, people who you can learn positive habits from. I like to go to seminars, workshops, toastmasters and boot camps to be around the right people. I do find lots of people on a similar journey, we all have a good time.

Next, systematize your decision making. By doing this, you can take decision making out of the process, leaving more mental room for bigger and better thinking. So, if you know that you ask the yourself same questions each day, write down the question and your best answer, and use that answer every time without thinking about it. For example "What's for dinner?" I would have a menu plan for the week. So I don't need to ask that question.

For what other decisions could you use this? Write them down now!! Or keep a pen and note pad handy so, you can jot down the questions. So you can systematize your decision making

Ask yourself how the work you do affects others? We all transform, other people whether we are conscious of it or not. So, think about how you will be helping someone else with their motivation. You starting to work on your goal or project could spark someone else to pull the trigger on theirs, which leads to teaching others.

Inspiring Others to Be Positive

The best way to learn something is to teach others. So, by learning to be positive, you can teach your partner, child, friends, or even a stranger, since you are now already leading a positive life. Use techniques and skills you have developed here, to lead by example.

ABCs to a Positive Life

Here are some ways to remind you:

- Find your own joy to make others happy and positive. What makes you happy? What brings you joy?

- Get your life in order. To help others, your own life messes should be in order. Your inspiration will have a greater impact on them. Also, your personal experiences might help the other person to be inspired to change their life to a more positive one.

- Aim for improving one's life, not perfecting it. While the first steps towards helping others is helping yourself, be careful not to put off the start for too long. Otherwise, you may not get started. Even if it is something small it will help.

- Identify your skills and talents. If you are trying to figure out how you can make a positive impact on the world, you should know as much about yourself as possible. What are you really good at? Are you a good organizer? Are you a natural at public speaking? Do you know computers, or how to use your smart phone effectively? Are you a good runner? Do you have hobbies that you can teach others? Can you build things?

- Think about how you work best. Just as you should know what you are good at, you should think about the type of environment you work best in. Do you thrive in an outdoor setting? Do you like an office setting? Do you like to work at home or out on the road?

- Be honest about what you truly enjoy, to keep yourself from boredom and burn-out. Make sure that you are doing is something you're good at and enjoy. For example, if you are a great writer, you could do well at writing a book, or blogs etc. But if you don't like to write, then it could become a burden if you were to do it full time as a way of making money. Doing what you are good at, and enjoy will be a great experience and will keep you going for a long time, which is what passion is all about.

Knowing Your Best Points/Self-Assessment

What is self-assessment? There are some people who would view self-assessment as an exam but it's actually not a test. There is no right or wrong answers that will tell you that you have conducted a self-assessment well. The real measure of a successful self-assessment is when you have successfully known yourself, your capabilities, interest, values, and even your personality type.

Knowing your best points is taking stock of all the things you like, enjoy and are good at. This is where you will list all of the things you like, enjoy, and are good at. Make this enjoyable, and have some fun with your lists. This list will help you reach your goals and contribute to your positive life. To make the self-assessment more effective, make sure that you reflect on your accomplishments, and back them up with evidence. Listed below are some steps you can take.

1. Set some time aside
2. Review your goals
3. Catalog you accomplishments
4. Keep the focus on you
5. Explain your struggles
6. Explain your growth
7. Assemble feedback from others
8. Keep it positive when writing

Here are some questions you can ask yourself:

- What do you enjoy?
- What are you good at?
- What success have you had to date?
- What awards or ribbons have you received?

- What's your personality type? (you can do an assessment on line)
- What are your weaknesses?
- What are your future goals?
- What are your present goals?

Let's take out a pen and paper now and write theses great things down......

Check out my website for examples at...www.thepositivelifebook.com

Great job on completing your assessment!!!

Chapter 9

Knowing Your Finish Line

"The world is full of people who have dreams of playing at Carnegie Hall, of running a marathon, and of owning their own business. The difference between the people who make it across the finish line and everyone else is one simple thing: an action plan."
John Tosh

In this chapter we will be making your action plan, to finding the path to get your goals accomplished, and making a map to your future positive life.

Finding Your Goals

So, if you finished your self-assessment, you should be close to knowing what your goals are. Let's work on your personal goals here. What dreams or expectations do you have? Setting goals allows you to plan how you want to move through life. Some goals can take a lifetime; others can be completed in a day or in a week. By setting goals and planning to achieve them, you will feel a sense of accomplishment and self-worth. That is a great feeling.

What are your life goals? Ask yourself some questions about what you want for your life. What do you want to achieve today? In a year? In your lifetime? What can you attain in 5, 10,m 15, 20 years from now? The answers to these questions can be as general as "I want to be happy" or "I want to help people."

You can break your goals up to categories, For example:

- Career - I want to open my own business and be successful.
- Fitness - I want to run a Tough Mudder every year.
- Personal - I want to have a happy family.
- Spiritual - I want to be a Catholic.
- Financial - I want to live debt free and be finically free.
- Education - I want to learn French.

Let's break the big picture down into smaller and more specific goals. Let's look at areas of your life that you either want to change or feel you would like to develop with time: career, finances, family, education, and health. Begin to ask yourself questions about what you would like to achieve in each area, and how you would like to approach each area with in a 5 - year time frame.

Now that you have a rough idea of what you want to accomplish within the next few years, make concrete goals to start working on that now. Give yourself a deadline, within a reasonable time frame. For short-term goals, under a year, make sure you write your goals down. This will help you be accountable for them. So, an example of a fitness goal would be to become fit. To make it specific, with a deadline, it would be that you I will be able to run 5k in 3 months. You will use a 5k app to help you achieve this goal. You are committed to follow this program for 3 months. Also, add a date to the goal; so if someone were to look at your goal, they would know when you complete it.

Apply this to each of your major goals, and make it happen!

You will need to adjust your goals periodically. You may find that you have accomplished some of your short-term goals, like your fitness goal of running 5k. Now you need to adjust that goal to the next level; for example, getting a better time in your 5k run, or starting to run 10k, or half a marathon or even a marathon, which will be part of your long-term goals.

Keep track of your progress. Writing in a journal is a great way to keep track of both personal and professional progress. Checking in with yourself, and acknowledging the progress made toward your goals, will help you to stay motivated and even make you work harder. You can also use a friend to help you stay focused. If you were training for your 5k, they could run with you or on the side lines cheering you on or even just talk about your progress.

Assess your goals. Make sure that when you have reached a goal, you allow yourself to celebrate accordingly. Take this time to assess the goal process, from beginning to end. You could review your running times, and frequency, and what you put in your journal to reflect on how you were feeling during the months of running.

So from the 5 k example, you could celebrate that goal by taking a week break from running, before you would get going to accomplish your next goal of a 10k run.

Keep setting goals. Once you have reached one level of your goals, keep on setting new goals. As in the example, once you have done your 10k run, you could better your run times, or the number of runs in a year. You could decide to do a triathlon or a 25 k mud run for, an example. The choice is yours, to keep getting better.

Knowing Your Route

"I see my path, but I don't know where it leads. Not knowing where I'm going is what inspires me to travel it."
Rosalia de Castro

Now that you have your goals set up, let's look at your route to get there. Much like setting up a GPS to get to a destination, you need some information. First, identify your starting point. Are there stops along the way? What type of transportation method are you going to use? Are there other routes that are available? Select your route and, finally, plan your route.

Step 1
What is your destination? In the above example of running, your ending point was a marathon.

Step 2
Where is your staring point? You could ask yourself some questions such as, how fit am I now? Do I need to have a physical? Where can I fit my run times into my schedule. In this step, don't over-whelm yourself with too many questions.

Step 3
What's your transportation method? How are you going to get to your destination? Are you going to do it on your own? Are you going to use a running app or get a coach? Each of these methods will get you to our destination, but it depends on how fast you want to get to the end. It's clear that having a coach would be the fastest way.

Step 4
Select and plan your route. Now that you have your destination, starting point, and the transportation method, let's plan your route. There is a quote that says, " It's funny how, day by day, nothing changes, but when you look back, everything is different." One year

from now, you will be one year older, no matter what. What can you do with your goals today that will make looking back feeling really different and really satisfying?

Keeping a journal of your goals and your progress will help keep you going throughout your journey. Also, make up a vision board of your goals, to help visually remind yourself too.

Drawing Your Map

Here is a system that is like a map, to help plot out your goals. The S.M.A.R.T. goal system is great. The letters stand for:

Specific – Write out clear and concise goals.
Goals are not ambiguous. Rather, you need to have a clear, concise goal that you can set your sights on. For example, rather than saying "I want to have a better body," you could say, " I want to lose fifteen pounds this summer." You can see how the example is more specific, and it is a better goal.

Measurable – The ability to track your progress.
Tracking the progress of your goals is an important part of keeping you motivated. It allows you to set milestones, which you can celebrate when you meet them, or revaluate when you don't. It's a good idea, to always have some aspect of your goal that can be measured and evaluated.

Achievable – Set challenging; yet achievable goals.
Far too many people fall into the trap of setting impossible goals for themselves. While impossible goals may push you forward for a while, you will almost certainly end up giving up on them at some point in the future. Instead of impossible, your goals should be challenging yet achievable.

Before you set a goal, make sure that you can actually envision yourself achieving it.

Relevant – Set goals that are relevant to your overall life plan.
Not all goals are as worthwhile as others. Unless your goal is relevant to your overall plan for your life, achieving it may not accomplish anything. In order to ensure that your goal is beneficial, make sure that it is worth your time. Make sure that achieving it will provide positive benefits to your life, and make sure that this goal aligns, at some degree, with other goals that you have.

Time – Have a target finishing time attached to your goals.
Good goals need to have a target time attached to them. For example, rather than saying , "I want to start reading more books" you could say, " I want to read ten books in the next six months." You can see how the second goal would be much more motivating to succeed, since they have a target date in mind for their goal.
When writing SMART goals, it is a good idea to write down each of the criteria. Then write a sentence or two about how your goal fits each one. If you can write a goal that fits each of these criteria, you will have come up with a SMART goal that is sure to be much more beneficial than a standard goal.

Let's look at some examples.

Saving Money

Let's say that your long term goal is to start saving more money. This goal can be modified so that it is a smart goal. You could say that you want to save $10,000 a year for the next ten years. Now, the goal is specific and measurable, since you have an amount that you are shooting for and the ability to measure the amount you end up actually saving. This goal is time-bound as well, since your goal is to save a specific amount each year over a given period. Whether the goal is achievable depends on your own financial situation, but

ABCs to a Positive Life

assuming it is, the goal fits that criteria as well. This goal fits all the criteria of being a smart goal.

Let's look at a short term goal, such as getting an A on a test.

Let's say you are a student and have a goal to get an A on an upcoming test. So, by using the SMART goal, you would fill each of the criteria,

S – to get an "A" on my upcoming math test
M – it is measureable by getting an "A"
A – it is achievable by repetition
R – by studying, I will understand and remember the material
T – Time, the date on the upcoming test

This is a smart goal from the start. By filling in the SMART goal acronym it will help you achieve the goal.

Now that you know where your finish line is, let's go to the winners circle!!!

Chapter 10

You Are a Winner

"Winners make a habit of manufacturing their own positive expectations in advance of the event."
Brian Tracy

Here we are at the last chapter. You are a winner! What does that mean? A winner is someone who accepts a win or a loss with the same temperament. A winner is never alone in winning a game, it's the people who stood by him/her that makes them a winner.

In this chapter, you will be congratulating yourself. Make sure you are maintaining your beliefs that you set up in the previous chapters, working on a routine for the morning and at the end of the day. Being a winner is about achieving goals and cultivating a winner's attitude. By setting goals and tracking your progress, treating your mind and body well, and surrounding yourself with positive influences. You are a winner!!

Here is an inspiring story for you. There is a man named Karoly Takacs. You may or may not know his name. He is from Hungary and he's is a national hero there. In 1939, Karoly Takas was in the Hungarian army, and he was the top pistol shooter in the world. He was going to compete in the 1940 Olympic Games scheduled for Tokyo. He was expected to take gold. Those expectations vanished one terrible day just months before the Olympics. While training with his army squad, a hand grenade exploded in Takacs' right hand, and his shooting hand was blown off.

Takas spent a month in the hospital depressed at both the loss of his hand and the end of his Olympic dream. At that point most people would have quit. They would have probably spent the rest of their life feeling sorry for themselves, but not Takacs. Takacs was a winner. Winners know that they can't let circumstances keep them down. They understand that life is hard and that they can't let life beat them down. Winners know in their heart that quitting is not an option.

Takacs did the unthinkable; he picked himself up, dusted himself off, and decided to learn how to shoot with his left hand. His reasoning was simple. He simply asked himself, why not?

Instead of focusing on what he didn't have, a world class right shooting hand, he decided to focus on what he did have. Incredible mental toughness, and a healthy left hand that, with time, could be developed to shoot like a champion. For months Takacs practiced by himself. No one knew what he was doing. Maybe he didn't want to subject himself to people who most certainly would have discouraged him from his rekindled dream.

In the spring of 1939, he showed up at the Hungarian national pistol shooting championship. Other shooters approached Takacs to give him their condolences and to congratulate him on having the strength to come watch them shoot. They were surprised when he said. "I didn't come to watch; I came to compete." They were even more surprised when Takacs won!

The 1940 and 1944 Olympics were cancelled because of World War II. It looked like Takacs' Olympic dream would never have a chance to realize itself. But Takacs kept training and in 1944 he qualified for the London Olympics. At the age of 38, Takacs won the gold medal and set a new world record in pistol shooting. Four years later, Takacs won the gold medal again at the 1952 Helsinki Olympics. Takacs was a man with the mental toughness to bounce back from anything.

Winners in every field have a special trait that helps them become unstoppable. A special characteristic that allows them to survive major setbacks on the road to success. Winners recover quickly. Bouncing back is not enough. Winners bounce back quickly. They take their hit, they experience their setback, they have the wind taken out of their sails, but they immediately recover. Right away they force themselves to look at the bright side of things. They say to themselves, "That's OK. There is always a way. I will find a way." They dust themselves off, and pick up where they left off.

The reason quick recovery is important is that if you recover quickly, you don't lose your momentum and your drive. Takacs recovered in only one month. If he had wallowed in his misery, if he had stayed under the circumstances, if he had played the martyr, and felt sorry for himself much longer, he would have lost his mental edge and he never would have been able to come back.

When a boxer gets knocked down, he has ten seconds to get back up. If he gets up in eleven seconds, he loses the fight. Remember that next time you get knocked down.

Takacs definitely had a right to feel sorry for himself. He had a right to stay depressed and to ask himself "Why me?" For the rest of his life, he had to the right to act like a mediocre man. Takacs made the decision to dig deep inside and find a solution. To pick himself up and to learn to shoot all over again. Winners always search for a solution. Losers always search for an escape.

Next time you get knocked down, decide you will act like a winner. Get up quickly, take action, and astound the world!

Maintain Your Beliefs

Beliefs are the principles that drive your actions in life, and help you make sense of the world around you. For the most part, your early beliefs were influenced by the people around you, like your parents, and, your friends, and even TV personalities began to influence your belief system. If you want to develop your own beliefs, you must first become aware of your pre-existing beliefs, and decide if they are helpful. Let's explore some ideas.

Label your core values. What are your personal values? An important part in developing your belief system is figuring out what you stand for, and your values are basically the causes you consider important. You can pinpoint your personal values by reflecting on times when you felt happiest, most proud, or satisfied. What was happening during these times? Try to label the factors that contributed to these feelings. Try reflecting exercises, like the assessment inventory you did in an earlier chapter.

You may need to take some time to yourself to become aware of the beliefs that drive your life. It could be as easy as isolating yourself at home, away from others for a day or a few hours. It could be a weekend getaway.

During this time, spot the connection between your thoughts and actions. You can use this model to help with the thought process. First, how did the event happen? For example a teacher yells at you for submitting an assignment late.

Second, what was your belief? For example, You think, "I cannot do anything right."

Thirdly, what was the consequence? For example, you don't try as hard to get things turned in on time.

From this example, you can see how this is a negative belief. A good way to start to change your thoughts is by. Start a new journal labelled "My Thoughts." In this journal, write your thoughts and beliefs down. It's a great way to recognize your thought patterns and to be able to change them into more positive and rewarding beliefs. You may find some negative ideas that you didn't know you had. This could help you get over some of them during your journalism time. Take time to challenge your interpretation of your beliefs. Then keep the helpful and rational ones. You could have them set up as reminders around your room to reinforce them.

Some examples such as "I can't do anything right" is a negative belief. You could search for possible solutions, such as, "I need to work harder," or "I need to developed better time management skills."

By re-framing your beliefs, you can ensure that your new belief system will be positive and growth oriented, which is what we want in our lives.

Making Your Morning Routine

Let's get some ideas for your morning routine. When you start your day right by having a routine that is positive and active, it will put you in the right frame of mind, which will carry you through the day.

Here is a routine I like. It's called the Bruce Lee challenge. In is a 5 step program created by Travis McShane.

- Step 1 is to identify the goals you want to achieve and break them down into little actions that you can take daily in order to reach them.

- Step 2 is where you reduce your goal to manageable bite-size pieces, and come up with a way to measure how you are doing with it. For instance, isn't it enough to say that you will incorporate exercise into your morning routine? You have to be specific, like deciding that you will walk on the treadmill for 20 minutes or that you will do 50 sit ups, 50 push-ups, and 100 jumping jacks.

- Step 3 consists of mentally committing to your goal for 21 days (roughly the amount of time that many believe it takes to make the actions a habit).
- Step 4 Is actually taking action toward your goal now, not tomorrow or next week.
- Step 5 is when you review the previous 21 days, and decide whether or not to continue with your new habit (which should be a resounding YES!!).

Here are some common morning routines that successful entrepreneurs have:

- Eat a good breakfast.
- Listen to your body clock.
- Do creative work when it feels best.
- Set an alarm to wake up, and an alarm to get to sleep.
- Disengage, with zero notification from apps and phones at night.
- Develop a morning routine that works on weekends too.
- Track your habits to better understand yourself.
- Finally, keep evolving your routine. Have a written copy in place that will keep you on track.

My current routine is like this: Lay out clothes for next day, get my lunch ready, wake up at 3am, drink a glass of water, have some toast and a green smoothie, do my stretching routine, do 50 push-ups, 50 sit-ups, and 10-15 chin ups. I will spend half an hour to forty five minutes writing, reading, or learning how to better myself. I will do a few minutes of journaling for gratitude, to finish up, and then I go to work.

My evening routine is not as scheduled: Give my family some hugs and kisses, my dog some pets, eat dinner, play with my daughter and dog, get daughter ready for bed, spend some time with wife talking about our days at work and other fun things.

What routine will you do? Create your own routine that matters to you, so you can achieve a better and improved life.

End of Day Winner Circle of Greatness

At the end of the day, how do you feel? Did you get all your tasks done? These are just some questions you might ask yourself. Let's set up an end-of-day winner circle of greatness. This is an end-of-day routine that will set you up for your greatness for the evening and the next day. With the routine, it should keep you up on details of your job, reduce overwhelm, and keep you feeling empowered and happy.

Here is an example that will help give you an idea of what you can do:

- Clean your desk. Put all pens, books, papers, and things away. Make sure everything is tidy. Wipe your desk down so that everything is clean and clutter free.

- Create your to-do list for tomorrow. Take some time to sit and write down everything you want to accomplish the next day. For example (for me), reply to certain emails, work on a project, design a cover for my new book, and write a report for my blog post. Keep the list simple, and focus on the things that have to be done in order to move your business and projects forward.

- Create your wish list. Keep a separate list where you can track your non-urgent wish list items. These may be things you would like to do down the road but don't want to forget about. Include those awesome ideas that come to mind, and anything else you want to capture and come back to later.

- By ending the day writing your lists, your brain dumps everything that is on your mind (which will help you sleep better at night). Your will feel like you accomplished something, and you will have closure at the end of the day. This will help you to feel more present, which will help with whatever you do next. (If you have a family, they would be very appreciative.)

- Keep a firm time for ending your workday. An alarm will help. Forgive yourself for not finishing everything. Give gratitude.

When do you know you are destined to do or be something great?

Actually when we are younger everyone feels they have and unlimited potential to do great things with our lives. However, over time society overwhelms us with discouraging ideas, to the point where we stop believing in ourselves. Well you need to know that you have greatness in you. No matter whom you are, if you're a human being living today you have greatness in you – you just have to start believing it. There are certain things that you can do and factors that will show you that you are heading in the right direction.

- You're resourceful: do you seem to figure out a way to make things happen, no matter what you're faced up against? That's a sign you're naturally resourceful, an incredibly useful skill for achieving virtually everything in life.

- You're a natural problem-solver: You were practically made to be an entrepreneur. That's because problem-solving is critical to virtually everything we do, from overcoming common day-to-day challenges that hinder your productivity to figuring out that next big business idea by identifying problems and thinking of creative solutions in the form of a product or service.

- Nothing stops you from accomplishing your goals: Are you the kind of person who always finishes what they start? If you always complete what you set out to do no matter what happens, and never allow yourself to settle or quit on your goals, you possess on of the most valuable qualities a person can have.

- You are relentlessly persistent. Are you the kind of person who gets up every time you get knocked down, and pushes forward through rain or shine? Persistence is a quality that virtually all wildly successful people display. The level of rejection, failure, and setbacks one inevitably faces has to be weathered in order to achieve greatness. Persistence helps you maintain the energy necessary to get there.

- You're not afraid of asking questions. Self-development requires that you be willing and unafraid to ask questions. It's as simple as that. If you're kind of person who isn't afraid to raise your hand in class room setting, and you possess the willingness to step outside of your comfort zone. You are bound for greatness.

- You never fail. B not failing, I'm referring to not viewing failure as a setback. If you treat failure like a building block, a valuable learning experience that moves you further forward towards your dreams and goals, then you may very well be bound for greatness. This is easily one of the most important qualities of all, so if this doesn't naturally describe you, don't worry; it's a quality you can develop with time and effort. Just look for the lessons in each "failure" to see what you can take away.

- You understand that change is in your hands. Many believe that people and the world at large can't be changed, that we're all somehow stuck blowing in a great big wind called fate and have little to no say about what happens to us. This is a damaging belief and fundamentally wrong. If you understand that change is in your hands, that's a healthy sign you're destined for greatness because you understand that you have your hands on the wheel, and naturally look for ways to improve and move forward. You can decide to make a difference not only in your own life, but also in the life of others.

Enjoy your end-of-day winner circle of greatness.

Congratulations

Let's congratulate you. You have made it to the end of the positive life book, a simple guide to a winning mindset. Look at some of your successes so far. What were they? Have you rewarded yourself effectively? Have you adopted a positive life style?

Congratulations! What a remarkable accomplishment. Just completing this book is something to brag about. You did it! Well done!

Keeps the moment going. Make sure to revisit some of the chapters that have inspired you to live a more positive lifestyle. Make sure your morning routine is a great one for you. Keep your mind active with brain games and reading some great books. You can keep on winning! I am happy to see that you are part of the positive lifestyle family. Please visit www.thepositivelifebook.com, and the positive lifestyle Facebook page.

I am sure there must have been many times when you wanted to give up, or when spending time doing other things may have seemed more attractive then read this great book, but your hard work and diligence have certainty paid off.

You will keep achieving great things in your life. Keep up the good work!! Lifting the Positive Lifestyle

About the Author

Curtis Leong is a new entrepreneur. He is entering a new chapter in his life. He is the author of the upcoming book ABCs of a Positive Life, the Simple Guide to a Winning Mindset. Has current finished Raymond Aaron's speaker course, and he is also a member of the 10-10-10 program. Curtis believes that through his personal trials, he has been able to maintain a positive attitude, and remain a fit and helpful member of the church.

Curtis has a 3rd degree black belt in taekwondo do. He has done several Tough Mudders, 2 Spartan races, and several other obstacle races in the past 5 years. He enjoys going to the gym, 3 times a week, and eating clean.

Curtis enjoys inspirational books by Bob Proctor, Robert G. Allen, Robert Kawasaki, Brian Tracey, Joe Vitale, Tony Robbins, Raymond Aaron, and serval others.

Curtis is honest, diplomatic, and motivated, and is a get-things done kind of guy who is being coached by Achieve Today. His current book *ABC's to a Positive Life* is his wealth of knowledge that he has gained over the years of working with people. His views, techniques, and life stories, which have been developed over time, are expressed in this book. His intention for you is to be able to use the tools that are presented in the book, to help you find your positive lifestyle, and to influence others to find theirs.

You can contact him at www.thepositivelifebook.com and www.curtis-cafe.com, thepositivelifebook@gmail.com

www.ingramcontent.com/pod-product-compliance
Lightning Source LLC
Chambersburg PA
CBHW050649160426
43194CB00010B/1874